Praise for *What If Everybody Understood Child Development?* by Rae Pica

"What a pleasure to read commonsense wisdom about what young children need!"

Diane Ravitch, Research Professor of Education
New York University

"This amazing book does far more than chase down the myths about how to ensure that children are successful. It offers real, research-backed practical strategies every teacher and parent can use. This belongs on every desk for quick and handy use!"

Eric Jensen, Director
Jensen Learning, Maunaloa, HI

"This book is a must read for anyone who is part of the current education system. It is time to think about what we are doing to the youth who are the new digital generation era and to ensure we are teaching them in ways that are the most developmentally appropriate."

Lyneille Meza, Coordinator of Data and Assessment
Denton ISD

"This is a great read. Its social media flavor is inviting and inspiring. The issues presented echo teacher discussions made around the water fountain. [Rae Pica's] expertise and evidence based on research will move your hair-pulling complaints to policy-changing action."

Leonard J. Villanueva, Teacher
Palisades Elementary School

"This book offers provocative ideas for the new educator, the experienced teacher, and administrators alike. Let's use what we know about child development to start remaking our schools to meet the needs of all students. This book provides a starting point."

Katrina L. Ladopoulos, Teacher
Crestwood Elementary School

"Rae Pica has a deep understanding of childhood development and she has delved into every facet of it so that educators, parents, and policymakers will come to that understanding too. *What If Everybody Understood Child Development?* includes 29 critically important chapters that focus on every single important issue we don't always take enough time to talk about. This book needs to not just be on everyone's shelves, but open in everyone's hands."

Peter DeWitt, Author/Consultant
Former K–5 Principal, Finding Common
Ground Blog—Education Week

"Our understanding of young children has become quite distorted, as have our policies and practices. It's time to reorient our views and Rae Pica's *What If Everybody Understood Child Development?* gives clear examples of the problems and of the solutions. To her, children are remarkable human beings—active, caring, and creative. They are more than an investment in the future. They are of immense value here and now."

Joan Almon, Co-Founder
Alliance for Childhood

"Rae Pica's *What If Everybody Understood Child Development?,* in its so readable and so interesting format, is an important contribution to a field that is constantly fighting to have facts about child development guide and inform decision making about young children rather than let the 'theory of the day' do harm to our youngest learners. I love, love, love this book!"

Marcy Guddemi, Executive Director
Gesell Institute

"Rae Pica understands children. With her wisdom and insight, she helps us know how to do right by kids in a world full of conflicting pressures. Thank you, Rae, for this valuable book. We need it now more than ever!"

Nancy Carlsson-Paige, Professor Emerita
Lesley University

What If Everybody Understood Child Development?

*This book is dedicated to my oldest friend, Sheila Chapman,
who has known me since we were thirteen and
still loves me these many years later.*

What If Everybody Understood Child Development?

Straight Talk About Bettering Education and Children's Lives

Rae Pica

CORWIN
A SAGE Company

CORWIN
A SAGE Company

FOR INFORMATION:

Corwin

A SAGE Company

2455 Teller Road

Thousand Oaks, California 91320

(800) 233-9936

www.corwin.com

SAGE Publications Ltd.

1 Oliver's Yard

55 City Road

London EC1Y 1SP

United Kingdom

SAGE Publications India Pvt. Ltd.

B 1/l 1 Mohan Cooperative Industrial Area

Mathura Road, New Delhi 110 044

India

SAGE Publications Asia-Pacific Pte. Ltd.

3 Church Street

#10-04 Samsung Hub

Singapore 049483

Printed in the United States of America

ISBN: 978-1-4833-8184-8

This book is printed on acid-free paper.

Acquisitions Editor: Jessica Allan

Senior Associate Editor: Kimberly Greenberg

Editorial Assistant: Cesar Reyes

Production Editor: Melanie Birdsall

Copy Editor: Grace Kluck

Typesetter: C&M Digitals (P) Ltd.

Proofreader: Susan Schon

Cover Designer: Gail Buschman

Marketing Manager: Amanda Boudria

Certified Chain of Custody
Promoting Sustainable Forestry
www.sfiprogram.org
SFI-01268

SFI label applies to text stock

15 16 17 18 19 10 9 8 7 6 5 4 3 2 1

Contents

"We have a tendency in this country to put everybody into a formula—throw them all into the same box and have these expectations that they're all going to do the same thing at the same time," stated Jane Healy, in an interview for BAM Radio Network, but "one size fits all" does not apply to children.

Whether we're talking about academics or athletics, the idea that earlier is better has infiltrated American society and education. As a result, there's been a pushdown in curriculum, and children are expected to read as babies and to play like Beckham years before their eye-foot coordination allows them to successfully connect foot to ball.

Being a passive receptacle and being required to perform in ways for which they're not developmentally ready creates children who come to resist—and even detest—"education." Learning that is joyful, on the other hand, creates a love of learning that an individual will retain for a lifetime.

opportunities for free play. They're too busy being scheduled and supervised and "schooled"—all of which are considered more important than something as "frivolous" as play.

14. The Body Matters, Too

Should the physical fitness of children be the concern of teaching professionals? Or is it a matter for the family, and the family alone, to worry about? First Lady Michelle Obama believes it's the former. And, given the alarming facts surrounding the childhood obesity crisis, I have to agree with her.

15. Reading, Writing, 'Rithmetic . . . and Recess

It's estimated that approximately 40 percent of the elementary schools in the United States have eliminated recess from the children's day—primarily because there are so many standards to be met and tests to be taken. It might be a reasonable choice if (a) standards and tests were all that mattered in a child's education, (b) children consisted of heads only, and (c) research didn't confirm that children can't afford *not* to have recess.

16. Why Kids Need "Gym"

I hated "gym" when I was a kid. But life can be funny; despite that, I became a children's physical activity specialist—and ended up teaching physical education (PE) majors. Also, despite that, I believe that all schoolchildren—but most especially those in the earliest grades—should have PE class—preferably daily. And I'll tell you why.

Part III. Understanding Developmentally Appropriate Practice

17. In Defense of Authentic Learning

Rote learning has its place. However, unless a child is going to grow up to become a contestant on television game shows, memorizing facts will have little use in life once she or he has passed all of the tests school requires. On the other hand, authentic learning—the process of exploration and discovery, of acquiring knowledge, or knowing *how* to acquire it—will serve a child endlessly.

Preface

In April 2013, I wrote a piece for *Huffington Post* called "What If Everybody Understood Child Development?" because I was fed up with the many ridiculous actions taken against children in the name of education or safety. What if all administrators, policymakers, educators, and parents really understood children—how they develop and what can be expected of them at certain stages? Surely children's lives would be so much better! Surely their education would be greatly improved.

Writing the piece was a necessity for me. I was asking a question that had been gnawing at me for some time. What I expected was relief at putting the question out there. What I hoped was that educators, administrators, policymakers, and parents would take notice. What I hadn't predicted was the response both the question and the piece would receive.

As of today, the post has been shared widely on social media, acquiring, among other things, more than 2,500 Facebook shares and 23,000 Facebook likes. Recently, it was moved from *Huff Post Education* to *Huff Post Impact*, where it received renewed interest that began a whole new round of sharing.

Along those same lines, not long ago I tweeted images comparing an "inactive" brain when someone is sitting quietly versus that of a quite vibrant brain following 20 minutes of walking. My tweet stated, "For those who think sitting = learning, take a look." Within a few hours there had been over 150 retweets and favorites. To this day, the tweet is still receiving reactions.

The messages contained in my *Huff* piece and in my tweet clearly resonated, especially with teachers who want to see "their" opinions expressed, their thoughts and feelings validated, and who need support to advocate for what's right for children!

Because the messages resonated so strongly, I was inspired to write this book. I wanted to offer teachers all of the above. Additionally, I wanted to help inform those teachers, administrators, policymakers, and parents who remain uncertain about what *is* developmentally appropriate for children in early childhood class-rooms and through the elementary grades.

The need for a basic understanding of children and developmentally appropriate practice has never been greater, as

- the educational climate in this country continues to remove decisions from the hands of educators and to place decisions in the hands of those with little to no knowledge of either children or education.
- many young teachers entering the field have grown up, as have today's young students, with little opportunity to experience the benefits of play, risk-taking, active learning, and life without fear, technology, or academic accountability.
- society and the media continue to perpetuate myths ("earlier is better," "children must be protected from risk and mistakes," "we must 'give' children self-esteem") that harm childhood and result in far too many bad educational policies.

Traditionally, the necessary understanding of children and developmentally appropriate practice would come from textbooks and college courses. However, many preservice teachers still are not required to study child development prior to beginning their careers. Nor are administrators, parents, or policymakers required to be familiar with the basic tenets of child development. In today's society, with "overwhelmed" the new normal, even if those who work and live with kids were to realize the need for a better understanding of children, few have time to read a textbook—or perhaps even a traditional book—on the subject.

What If Everybody Understood Child Development? is not a "traditional" book. Consisting of 29 essays, all of which run approximately 900 to 1300 words in length, it meets the needs of today's busy readers who can easily and quickly read the pieces whenever time allows, in whatever order preferred.

The opinions expressed in these essays are based on my 35 years as an education consultant, but they're also supported by research, anecdotal evidence, stories shared by teachers and parents, and the views of experts in the fields of education, child development, play research, the neurosciences, and more—most of whom I have interviewed in my role as a radio host on BAM Radio Network. I feel as though my years as an educator, together with the unique opportunities I've had to speak with hundreds of thought leaders, led me inevitably to this project.

In addition to the thoughts expressed, each essay concludes with what the executive producer at BAM Radio calls "actionable insights"—recommendations for what you, as a teacher, parent, or education advocate, can do to help bring about change. Each also offers a short list of resources, including links to online articles and the appropriate radio segments, for those wishing to learn more about the topic at hand.

It's unlikely you'll agree with all of the opinions expressed here. But whether or not you agree, it's my hope that the straight talk in *What If Everybody Understood Child Development?* will inspire and motivate you to generate change—so children can begin to have the lives and education they deserve.

Acknowledgments

I can't begin to thank all of the people responsible, not only for making this book possible, but also for being part of my life's journey to this point. Among them are

- my partner in life, Fredrick Davis, whose belief in me knows no bounds;
- friends Patti Page, Jane Fitzpatrick, Jody Martin, and Dionne Gray, for their ongoing "life support;"
- Patriots' pals Kelly O'Meara, Kathleen Dwyer, and Bowen Spievack, who add considerably to the joy in my life;
- my mom, Eleanor Pica-Merrill, for being there when I need her;
- the fabulous team at Corwin, including Lisa Shaw, Executive Director, for welcoming me so warmly into the fold; Jessica Allan, Acquisitions Editor, who has proved to be a kindred spirit and a delight to work with; Production Editor Melanie Birdsall, for offering the kind of support every author dreams of; and Copy Editor Grace Kluck, for making the process painless;
- Errol Smith, who got me started on the journey that became BAM Radio Network and whose ideas and inspiration have led me down new paths, and Jeannette Bernstein Smith, whose efforts and support make my work for BAM easier and better;
- the many incredible experts I've interviewed for *Body, Mind and Child, Teacher's Aid,* and now *Studentcentricity*;
- the fabulous education professionals who have joined me on my interviews as commentators; and
- all of the education professionals and parents who have attended my keynotes and trainings and who have shared their stories with me.

Publisher's Acknowledgments

Corwin gratefully acknowledges the contributions of the following reviewers:

Sara B. Coleman
High School Science Teacher
Norwalk High School
Norwalk, IA

Ellen E. Coulson
Seventh-Grade
    U.S. History Teacher
Sig Rogich Middle School
Las Vegas, NV

Freda Hicks
Principal
Perry Harrison School
Pittsboro, NC

Tara Howell
Science Department and
    Advanced Studies
    Department Chair;
    Secondary Science Teacher
University City High School,
    San Diego Unified School
    District
San Diego, CA

Lyneille Meza
Coordinator of Data
    and Assessment
Denton ISD
Denton, TX

Diana Shepherd
Professor of Child Development
Department of
    Child Development
California State University,
    Chico
Chico, CA

Diane P. Smith
School Counselor
Smethport Area School District
Smethport, PA

Linda K. Taylor
Assistant Professor
Ball State University
Muncie, IN

Leonard J. Villanueva
Elementary School Teacher,
    Grade 2
Palisades Elementary School,
    Department of Education,
    State of Hawai`i
Pearl City, HI

Robert C. Wallon
Doctoral Student
University of Illinois at
    Urbana-Champaign
Champaign, IL

About the Author

Rae Pica has been an education consultant (www.raepica.com) specializing in the education of the whole child, children's physical activity, and developmentally appropriate practice since 1980. A former adjunct instructor with the University of New Hampshire, she is the author of 19 books, including the text *Experiences in Movement and Music,* in its fifth edition; the award-winning *Great Games for Young Children* and *Jump into Literacy*; and the parenting book, *A Running Start: How Play, Physical Activity and Free Time Create a Successful Child.* Rae is known for her lively and informative keynotes and trainings and has shared her expertise with such groups as the *Sesame Street* Research Department, the Head Start Bureau, Centers for Disease Control, the President's Council on Physical Fitness and Sports, Nickelodeon's *Blue's Clues*, Gymboree, Nike, and state health departments throughout the country. Rae also blogs for *Huffington Post*, is a member of the executive committee of the Academy of Education Arts and Sciences, and is cofounder of BAM Radio Network (www.bamradionetwork.com), the world's largest online education radio network, where she currently hosts *Studentcentricity*, interviewing experts in education, child development, play research, the neurosciences, and more.

Introduction

*What If Everybody
Understood Child Development?*

When writing my *Huffington Post* piece on children and gun play, I found myself wondering what would happen if everyone understood child development. What changes would come about in education? How much healthier would children's lives be if this unique period of their lives was fully understood?

Since then, here are a few of the things I've encountered:

- Another child, this time a seven-year-old, was suspended from school for biting his strawberry Pop Tart into the shape of a gun. Really?
- A mom responded to one of my tweets about project-based learning with a comment to the effect that she'd just objected to that "nonsense" in her son's science class (perhaps the content area most suited to inquiry learning).
- A mom sent me an e-mail pleading for help because her daughter, who has ADHD, is constantly having recess withheld because she forgets things.
- I read multiple stories of elementary school children not allowed to talk during lunch.
- A mom told me she prefers that her child do computer art because it's less messy than traditional art.

You might wonder why that last one is such a big deal. Well, anyone who understands child development knows that children learn and retain more when their senses are fully engaged. Manipulating a mouse and watching images transform on a screen can't begin to compare to dipping a paintbrush—or both hands—into a pool of color and slathering it onto surfaces with textures ranging from smooth to coarse, absorbent to impermeable, or to the satisfaction that comes from kneading and shaping malleable clay or Play-Doh, or to wrapping little fingers around a big, fat, promising crayon and immersing oneself in the self-expression only possible with seven shades of purple.

Anyone who understands child development—as the teachers and administrators at every school should—would know that withholding recess is not only futile (it doesn't work as a deterrent); also, it can be said to constitute cruelty. By now we should have heard enough about the childhood obesity crisis to understand the value of physical activity. Human beings—especially children—need to move. Neither the body nor the brain can function optimally without movement. In fact, sitting for more than ten minutes at a time increases fatigue and reduces concentration. And physical activity alleviates stress—something with which far too many children are living these days (often because the adults in their lives don't understand child development).

Still, when the above-mentioned mom took her case to her daughter's superintendent, principal, and teachers, she was told there would be no exceptions to their policy regarding the denial of recess to those who break the rules. Rules that included coming unprepared to class and leaving the classroom for a bathroom break! They even informed this mom that they could think of no deterrent other than a recess denial. Again: really, people?

As far as project-based learning is concerned, it may well be that those who were forced to sit in neatly aligned desks all day every day during their school years will see this approach as "nonsense." They were accustomed to having information force-fed to them only so that they could regurgitate it on tests. But anyone who understands child development—and brain-based learning—knows that pursuing one's interests results in truer, deeper learning. That hands-on, inquiry-based approaches stimulate the mind and the soul and will serve our children, now and in the future, far better than the expectation that there is only one right answer to every question.

And children prevented from talking to each other at lunch? I was witness to this several years ago (adults standing guard like Gestapo) and was dismayed to discover that what I thought was an aberration is in actuality a common practice in this day and age.

Where, I wonder, do such children learn to communicate? How do they learn to be part of a society? Certainly not in classrooms where they are instructed to keep their eyes, hands, and thoughts to themselves. Not on their way from the classroom to the cafeteria, where they're often hushed and/or threatened. Not at the one, brief recess they *may* get during the day. Not after school, in neighborhoods that have changed considerably since I was a kid, when most children are staring at one screen or another anyway. How is social development supposed to be fostered in environments such as these? Do we imagine that one grows up and suddenly knows how to effectively communicate and collaborate and to be part of a community?

A while back, I was part of a discussion on BAM Radio Network titled "Moving Toward Child Development Requirements for Teachers." Most people, I imagine, would be surprised to learn that understanding child development is not one of the standard requirements to become a teacher—or maybe not. Maybe most people, including those who decide what teachers need to know, are unaware of the incontestable connection between how children develop (not just cognitively but also socially, emotionally, and physically) and how they learn.

When I hear stories about teachers and administrators making decisions that create the impression they don't know children *at all*, I speculate about how different things might be if everyone understood child development. When I hear stories of small children who are bewildered, frustrated, and even defeated in their earliest school experiences, trying with brave determination to do what is asked of them and failing to understand why they can't, I wonder, *what if everybody understood child development?* At the very least, shouldn't every educator and school administrator?

PART I

Understanding Children

CHAPTER 1

All Children Are Not the Same

I t certainly seems to be one of those "duh" statements—all children are not the same. I mean, why would we imagine otherwise? If we accept that no two snowflakes are alike, why wouldn't we accept that no two individuals—even of the same age and gender—are alike? It's just plain common sense.

But common sense doesn't appear to translate to education policies.

In an interview on BAM Radio Network, noted early childhood expert Jane Healy said, "We have a tendency in this country to put everybody into a formula—to throw them all into the same box and have these expectations that they're all going to do the same thing at the same time."

For the most part, that's always been the case with education: expecting all children in the same grade to master the same work at the same level and pace. But since the inception of No Child Left Behind—and now with Race to the Top and the implementation of the Common Core Standards (*common* being the operative word)— it's only gotten worse. The "box" has gotten even smaller. And the younger the children, the less room there is for movement inside it (play on words intended).

There's nothing wrong with standards, or goals, per se. It makes sense to establish a certain level of mastery for children to achieve and to determine what students should be able to do and know over the course of a particular period of time, a school year, for example.

But the standards should be realistic. It should be possible for the majority of students to achieve them, each at her or his own pace. That means the standards must also be developmentally appropriate and based on the principles of child development—designed with actual children in mind.

But they're not. Standards are written by people with little to no knowledge of child development or developmentally appropriate practice. They're written with too little input from people who do have that knowledge, such as teachers and child development experts. In fact, of the 135 people on the committees that wrote and reviewed the K–3 Common Core Standards, not one was a K–3 teacher or an early childhood professional.

Of course, along with developmentally inappropriate standards comes developmentally inappropriate curriculum. David Elkind said the following in another BAM interview:

> We don't teach the college curriculum at the high school. We don't teach the high school curriculum at the junior high. We don't teach the junior high curriculum at the elementary level. Why should we teach the elementary curriculum at the pre-school level? . . . We have no research to support it; all the research is opposed to it, and yet we do it.

Teachers, more and more often, are being asked to teach in ways they know to be developmentally inappropriate. They're asked to make demands of students whom they know are not developmentally ready for such demands. And, as Jane Healy noted, "When you start something before the brain is prepared, you've got trouble."

If we're to give the standards and curriculum writers the benefit of the doubt, we could admit that children these days appear to be smarter and savvier than they used to be. But, according to Marcy Guddemi, executive director of the Gesell Institute of Child Development, children are not reaching their developmental milestones any sooner than they did in 1925 when Arnold Gesell first did his research.

As an example, demonstrating the large range of what is "normal" in child development, Marcy explains that the average age children learn to walk is 12 months—50 percent before and 50 percent after. But the *range* that is normal for walking is $8\frac{3}{4}$ months all the way to 17 months. The same applies for reading. The *average* age that children learn to read is six-and-a-half—again, 50 percent before and 50 percent after.

She told me in an interview, "One of our misguided expectations right now in the education field is that every child should leave kindergarten reading. Well, not every child is going to leave kindergarten reading."

But that doesn't mean the policymakers and standards writers won't continue to demand that they do.

Anyone who understands child development knows

- It's simply not possible for all children to do and know the exact same things at the exact same age.
- All children go through the exact same stages in the exact same order but they do it at varying rates.
- Each domain—cognitive, physical, emotional, social—has its own rate of development.

And here's the big one:

- A child's development absolutely cannot be accelerated or hurried in any way.

All of this has been proved by research. But those with common sense—or kids—don't need research to verify these facts. They simply need to look at any two siblings, even twins, and note the differences. When we consider the myriad possibilities for genetic combinations, along with various environmental factors, it's clear that we can't begin to envision the diversity in temperament, intellect, skills, and learning styles among a group of 30 children in the same classroom.

One of my favorite lines from the interview with David Elkind was, "Wrong ideas always seem to catch on more easily than right ones." The idea that all children are the same is definitely a wrong idea.

What's a Teacher to Do?

- Speak up. If people who *do* understand child development stay quiet as unrealistic expectations are foisted on children, we'll never see things change for the better. Write blog posts. Contribute comments to other people's blogs. Hold policymakers and standards writers accountable by posting any bit of nonsense you come across on Twitter and Facebook. Become a part of groups like Defending the Early Years so you don't stand alone. Write to your senators and congresspersons. Enlist the aid of parents and the local media.

- When it comes time to vote, whether it be for mayor, governor, congressperson, senator, or school board member, use your political power to *just say no* to those who don't stand for what's best for children.

- Support the children in your classroom. Watch and listen to determine the developmental level of each individual child—cognitively, socially, emotionally, and physically—and, as they say, meet the children where they are.

- Help parents understand that all children can't be expected to be the same. Explain that comparisons are futile. Reassure them that there's nothing to fear if their child isn't reading as early as other children. Tell them that by the end of third grade it's impossible to tell who read early and who read late because it has all evened out by then, and tell them about neurophysiologist Carla Hannaford who didn't read until she was ten.

Where to Learn More

- "How to Help Children Learn to Read Well" with Dr. Jane Healy

  http://www.bamradionetwork.com/educators-channel/161-how-to-help-children-learn-to-read-well

- "Giving Your Child the Very Best Head Start" with Dr. David Elkind

  http://www.bamradionetwork.com/parents-channel/131-giving-your-child-the-very-best-head-start

- "Are Children Smarter, Learning More, Sooner, Faster?"

  www.bamradionetwork.com/educators-channel/546-are-children-smarter-learning-more-sooner-faster

- "Is Your Child Developing Normally?"

  www.bamradionetwork.com/parents-channel/126-is-your-child-developing-normally

- "CCSS in Kindergarten for Boys"

  www.gesellinstitute.org/ccss-in-kindergarten-for-boys/

- Defending the Early Years

  www.deyproject.org

CHAPTER 2

The Earlier the Better?

A mother told me her son was seven months old when she first felt the pressure to enroll him in enrichment programs. She said, "Here I was with an infant who had just learned to sit upright by himself, and someone was asking me what classes he was going to be taking, as if he were ten!"

Another mom, an early childhood professional who understood child development, complained to me that she was under tremendous pressure to enroll her daughter in the local, competitive soccer program. When I asked her daughter's age, she replied, "Two and a half."

A few years back, the *San Francisco Chronicle* told the story of one woman who called a popular preschool to say she was thinking about getting pregnant and wanted to put her baby-to-be on the school's waiting list. I learned of another mother who enrolled her child in "preschool prep"—at four months old. *ABC Nightline* reported the story of a mom so determined that her daughter get into a "prestigious" preschool that she wrote to the Vatican, asking them to pen a letter of recommendation for the child's application.

What all of these stories—and many, many others like them—have in common is the belief that *earlier is better*. You just can't start kids too soon on the road to success. And it's not just parents who believe it. As stated by Nancy Bailey in an article titled "Setting Children Up to Hate Reading":

Politicians, venture philanthropists, and even the President, make early learning into an emergency. What's a poor kindergartener or preschooler to do when they must carry the weight of the nation on their backs—when every letter and pronunciation is scrutinized like never before?

Unfortunately, many kindergarten teachers have bought into this harmful message. Many have thrown out their play kitchens, blocks, napping rugs, and doll houses believing it is critical that children should learn to read in kindergarten!

Kindergarten, according to studies from the American Institutes for Research and the University of Virginia, has become "the new first grade." And, based on my observations, preschool has clearly become the new kindergarten. The directors and teachers in private preschools all around the country tell me that parents are putting increasing pressure on them to switch from play-based to academic-oriented curriculums. If the schools don't submit to the parents' wishes, they risk losing enrollment to those schools that do favor early academics.

The belief that earlier is better has become deeply ingrained in our society—whether we're talking about academics or athletics. Parents are terrified that if they don't give their little ones a jump-start on the "competition," their children will fall behind and end up as miserable failures. Politicians pander to the ridiculous notion that education is a race. And teachers—from preschool to the primary grades—are being forced to abandon their understanding of what is developmentally appropriate and teach content they know to be wrong for kids.

And what happens to the kids? They're too often stressed and miserable. Depression among children is at an all-time high. Children taught to read at an early age have more vision problems, and those taught to read at age five have more difficulty reading than those taught at age seven.

And of course reading isn't the only skill children are being asked to acquire too early; requirements in all content areas have risen as curriculum is "pushed down" from higher to lower grades. Anxiety rises as children fail to meet their parents' and teachers' expectations—because they're developmentally incapable of doing what's asked of them. All of this does nothing to endear them to learning.

On the athletic side, when foot-eye coordination isn't fully developed until the age of nine or ten and children just barely beyond the wobbling stage are being asked—no, *obliged*—to play soccer at practically professional levels, they're also set up to fail. Children asked to catch a small white ball hurtling through the air at them before their visual tracking skills are fully formed learn not to catch but to become fearful. Children whose growing muscles, joints, and bones are stressed beyond what should be expected of them risk injury—sometimes lifelong injury. All of this does nothing to endear them to physical activity.

So, whether we're talking about moving or learning, two things children are born loving, the end result is often the same: loss of motivation. Demanding that children perform skills for which they're not yet ready creates fear and frustration in them. Moreover, children who are "trained" by adults to develop at a pace that is not their own tend to become less autonomous people.

And here's the punchline: child development *cannot* be accelerated. Moreover, there's no reason to *try* to accelerate it. The research shows that usually by third grade, and certainly by middle school, there's no real difference in reading levels between those who started reading early and those who started later. The research shows that children who begin in sports when they're developmentally ready catch up to and even surpass those who started early.

As to the play-versus-academics debate in early learning, studies have also determined that children enrolled in play-oriented preschools don't have a disadvantage over those who are enrolled in preschools focusing on early academics. One study, in fact, showed that there were neither short-term nor long-term advantages of early academics versus play and that there were no distinguishable differences by first grade. In another study, fourth graders who had attended play-oriented preschools in which children often initiated their own activities had *better* academic performance than those who had attended academic-oriented preschools.

But no one in charge is paying attention to the research. Given that, here are some of the concerns I have:

- What's to ensure children won't be burned out from all the pushing and pressure before they've even reached puberty?
- If we've caused them to miss the magic of childhood, how will kids ever find the magic necessary to cope with the trials and tribulations of adulthood?

- What will become of the childlike nature adults call upon when they need reminding of the delight found in simple things—when they need to bring out the playfulness that makes life worth living?
- At what cost will all of this "pushing down" come?

Childhood is not a dress rehearsal for adulthood. It is a separate, unique, and very special phase of life. And we're essentially wiping it out of existence in a misguided effort to ensure children get ahead.

When did we decide that life was one long race? When, exactly, did life become a competition?

What's a Teacher to Do?

- Just say *no*. As I like to tell my audiences, there are more of us than them. We have the power—including the political power—to stop the insanity. Become involved in policy at whatever level you can. Sign online letters and petitions addressed to policymakers. Use social media to express your views about developmentally inappropriate practice. Join forces with groups such as Defending the Early Years because there's power in numbers in doing so. Refuse to vote for senators, congresspersons, governors, mayors, or school board members who do not support good education policy and practice.

- Invite policymakers to your classroom to see what developmentally appropriate instruction and learning look like.

- Get parents on your side. Educate them about the fallacies behind the belief that earlier is better. Don't be shy about pointing out the potential problems inherent in trying to hurry child development.

- Despite what's happening around you, plan your curriculum and use teaching practices based on the research, *not* on the nonsense being promoted by those who don't know any better.

Where to Learn More

- "Teaching Reading: When Is Too Early, When Is Too Late?"
  www.bamradionetwork.com/educators-channel/608-teaching-read-when-is-too-early-when-is-too-late

- "Is Your Child Developing Normally?"
  www.bamradionetwork.com/parents-channel/126-is-your-child-developing-normally

- Defending the Early Years
  http://deyproject.org/

- "A Very Scary Headline about Kindergartners"
  www.washingtonpost.com/blogs/answer-sheet/wp/2014/02/06/a-really-scary-headline-about-kindergarteners/

- "Setting Children Up to Hate Reading"
  http://nancyebailey.com/2014/02/02/setting-children-up-to-hate-reading/

CHAPTER 3

The Power of Joy

Music educator Emile Jaques-Dalcroze (1865–1950) claimed that joy is the most powerful of all mental stimuli.

It's an interesting contention, especially considering the many non-joyful stories I hear from educators and parents about children crying over tests, children with so much homework that there's little time for anything else, let alone joy, in their lives, children discouraged by schooling as early as kindergarten, and children who are stressed out, burned out, acting out, and dropping out. Oh yes, and popping antidepressants at an astonishing and alarming rate.

Sadly, none of that surprises me anymore. After all, what part of today's emphasis on accountability and academics screams *joy*? How much joy comes from prepping for test after test? How much joy do we witness from students bent over desks and filling in bubbles? How much joy is experienced by students whose success, along with their teacher's, depends on how well they do on those endless tests?

Granted, there isn't a whole lot of research to back up Dalcroze's contention—because there aren't many researchers who would have considered it a worthy topic. But there is some, including a recent study by two Finnish educators that points to several sources of joy in the classroom. They include

- active, engaged efforts from the children;
- desire to master the material—to become "expert" at something;
- students allowed to work at their own level and pace;

- finishing a task or solving a problem and the time to do so;
- the chance to make choices;
- sharing and collaborating with other students; and
- the opportunity to play.

We *do* have a great deal of research detailing the impact of *stress* on the learning process. Dr. William Stixrud sums it up quite nicely when he writes, "stress hormones actually turn off the parts of the brain that allow us to focus attention, understand ideas, commit information to memory and reason critically." Not a whole lot of learning going on when that happens. It's darn hard to think straight when your system is poised for fight-or-flight.

Despite this evidence (and it doesn't surprise me anymore that we ignore the evidence either), the policymakers just keep demanding practices that create more stress and suck the joy right out of school. Coincidentally, *as I was writing this piece*, our chief education policymaker, Secretary of Education Arne Duncan, posted a blog in which he wrote these words: "Too much testing can rob school buildings of joy, and cause unnecessary stress." His solution was a one-year reprieve on test-based teacher ratings.

I might forgive the policymakers for ignoring (or, if I'm giving them the benefit of the doubt—being unaware of) the research on the roles of stress and joy in learning, but Dalcroze clearly didn't need research to reach his conclusion. During his time, there was no Internet to allow for large-scale surveys or the collection of anecdotal evidence. There were no neuroimaging and brain mapping scans to reveal that more pleasure areas of the brain light up when individuals are undertaking tasks they enjoy.

I imagine he based his opinion on how *he* felt when learning something new or when he engaged in the act of creation. Perhaps he discovered that whenever he was fully engrossed in a project, he experienced what psychologist Mihaly Csikszentmihalyi calls "flow"—that wonderful occurrence when time passes without our noticing. Of being so involved in what we're doing that we're aware of nothing else. Each of us has gloried in such experiences on occasion—for example, in the act of writing, painting, cooking, or teaching.

Perhaps Dalcroze based his contention on the observation of children. He may well have observed them in the process of creating and learning. Watch any child involved in self-directed activity—whether it's trying to write their name for the first time, staging an elaborate production, or experimenting with a chemistry set—and you'll witness flow. There's no one more engaged—or engaging to watch—than children fully absorbed in an undertaking. They direct all of their attention and effort into it. They put their heart and soul into it. And, if required to stop, the upset is profound, because who wants to stop feeling joy?

Wholehearted absorption doesn't describe much about what kids—or teachers—are required to do in school these days. And that is such a shame.

Imagine the lost potential as students continue to struggle to learn when anxious and unhappy. Imagine the ever-increasing number of students stressed out, burned out, acting out, and dropping out if things don't turn around and quickly. Imagine the lost potential if students are kept from discovering the power of joy in the classroom.

Neurologist and teacher Judy Willis has written, "Joy and enthusiasm are absolutely essential for learning to happen— literally, scientifically, as a matter of fact and research. Shouldn't it be our challenge and opportunity to design learning that embraces these ingredients?"

What's a Teacher to Do?

• Be excited and joyful about the learning that takes place in your classroom. When you're excited, the children will be excited.

• As often as possible, use humor in the classroom to lighten things up. In a BAM Radio discussion, Diana Loomans said that when you have a laughing classroom you have students who are participating more, perform better, and retain more information. In that same segment, Ed Dunkelblau contended that humor, laughter, and play are pleasurable experiences that attract and engage students, making it easier to teach. He said, "Humor is one of the few educational strategies that does as much good for the teacher as it does for the students."

- To the extent possible, make test prep fun, rather than drudgery. For ideas, listen to "Ten Ways to Make Test Prep Fun" (see below).

- Employ the excellent suggestions in Steven Wolk's article, "Joy in School" (see below).

Where to Learn More

- "The Neuroscience Behind Stress and Learning"

  www.edutopia.org/blog/neuroscience-behind-stress-and-learning-judy-willis

- "Fostering Joy in the Classroom"

  http://anniemurphypaul.com/2014/03/fostering-joy-at-school-and-at-work/

- "Joy in School"

  www.ascd.org/publications/educational-leadership/sept08/vol66/num01/Joy-in-School.aspx

- "Using Humor to Get Students to the Top of Bloom's Taxonomy"

  www.bamradionetwork.com/teachers-aid/1991-using-humor-to-get-students-to-the-top-of-blooms-taxonomy

- "Ten Ways to Make Test Prep Fun"

  www.bamradionetwork.com/educators-channel/1873-ten-ways-to-make-test-prep-fun

- *The Laughing Classroom: Everyone's Guide to Teaching with Humor and Play* by Diana Loomans and Karen Kolberg

CHAPTER 4

Bubble Wrapping Not Required

"I walked or biked to school for years, but my children don't. I worry about the road. I worry about strangers. You can start to imagine evil on every corner. In some ways, I do think they're missing out. But I like to be able to see them, to know where they are and what they are doing," stated a mom in a newspaper article called "Bubble-Wrap Generation: Our Molly-Coddled Kids."

"[I don't know] one friend of mine who can actually walk across the street without parental supervision . . . Parents these days are completely paranoid!" wrote a 12-year-old girl in a letter to the editor of the *New York Times*.

"I worry about having stairs in the house because they're dangerous for the kids," said practically every parent searching for a new place to live on HGTV's *House Hunters*. They also look at fenced-in yards from the vantage of the kitchen window and sigh in relief because they'll be able to observe their children at play while cooking. And they demand an open floor plan, not because they like to be able to entertain guests while prepping food but because they'll always be able to see their kids in the family room.

What is going on here? Surely through the ages children have been raised in homes with staircases and have survived! We might have a much smaller world population otherwise. Surely many of us remember playing, not just in the family room but in any darn room we chose, including the basement. Playing, not just in fenced-in yards but in entire neighborhoods. Walking—sometimes long distances—to school. And we did much of it without an adult in sight.

The insanity of it all struck me one day when a young mother approached me after a speech to ask if it was okay if she sometimes didn't play with her child. I stared at her blankly for a few moments. I honestly didn't know what she was asking. And then it hit me: she had gotten it into her head—either due to our society's scare tactics or to the current misguided notion that a good parent is an *always-involved* parent—that she had to spend 100 percent of her time with her child. That if her child was playing, she had to play with her.

I assured the mom that it was absolutely fine if she didn't constantly accompany her child in play. I cited some of the benefits of children playing on their own, and she seemed convinced. But I couldn't get her question out of my head. Worse, I couldn't get the image out of my head of what it would have been like had *my* mother been present during all of my childhood play experiences. I mean, I love my mother; but the idea of never being without her when I was a kid, well, it made me shudder.

Do you recall the elation of running freely with your friends? The glorious freedom of *not* being watched? Do you recall some of the risks you took? The giddy anticipation prior to taking a risk and the exhilaration of conquering it? How many of those adventures would you have bypassed had your mom been with you? For me, the answer is all of them.

To say we've become risk-aversive where children are concerned is a laughable understatement. And it's not just parents (who, arguably, are the easiest of groups to frighten). Teachers and school administrators, perhaps in reaction to parents' concerns and certainly in reaction to the fear of litigation, are showing the same symptoms. They're removing monkey bars and swing sets from school playgrounds. They're outlawing tag, cartwheels, and sometimes even running—and, oh yes, recess. In "A City With No Children," which appeared in *The Atlantic*, Kaid Benfield cited the story of a school district refusing to join the other 425 schools in the state participating in a national Walk to School Day. They insisted that walking to school is unsafe, regardless of how well planned or supervised it is.

These actions are beyond ridiculous. And they perpetuate the myth that there is danger everywhere—that children must be bubble wrapped in order to advance from infancy to adulthood in one piece.

I realize it's difficult to believe otherwise, especially considering the paranoia spread by the media's incessant tales of tragedy, presented in all their gory minutiae. But the experts—and there are many of them—insist that today's children are no less safe than children of my generation. Stranger danger, which tends to top the list of parents' fears, truly is a myth. According to the U.S. Department of Justice statistics on violent crimes, between 1973 and 2002, out of every thousand children kidnapped, just one or two of them were abducted by strangers. In fact, according to the National Center for Health Statistics, children are four times more likely to die of heart disease than to be kidnapped by a stranger.

That latter point bears emphasizing in light of the fact that much of the decline in risk-taking also involves a significant decline in physical activity in children's lives. Social historian Peter Stearns, quoted in a *Psychology Today* article called "A Nation of Wimps," backed up this argument rather nicely when he maintained that parents have exaggerated many of the dangers of childhood while overlooking others, such as the demise of recess.

Beyond the loss of physical activity and its related potential health problems, there is the disturbing description of today's bubble-wrapped children, made by a number of experts, as dependent, risk-aversive, psychologically fragile, and riddled with anxiety.

Doesn't sound much like a generation I trust to become strong and courageous adults.

Children are meant to be risk-takers. Mother Nature made them that way while also providing them with the ability to know just how far to push the boundaries. There are infinite benefits to kids being allowed to take the risks that nature intended. And there are infinite problems resulting from the lack of opportunity to take them. Kids who grow up afraid of risk will not be problem solvers. They will not be resilient. They will certainly not be able to handle risk, which is inherent in life, when it comes along. Many, in fact, will crumble. And children raised in a culture of fear—well, that's just asking for trouble.

Talk to any counselor at a college or university today, and they'll tell you that they've never seen more students unable to function on their own.

So, where's the real risk here?

What's a Teacher to Do?

- Educate, educate, educate. Parents only want the best for their children, and when they bubble wrap, they believe they're doing what's best. Help them to understand the benefits of allowing their children to take risks.

- Learn to be a "play worker" on the playground. These adults are knowledgeable about what constitutes real risk, but they don't hover or overprotect. They also manage to be watchful while remaining as invisible as possible.

- Watch your words. Whether in the classroom or on the playground, don't worry out loud about "scary" things. To the extent possible, bite back words of caution—especially with girls. In one study, parents issued more words of encouragement to sons ("You can do it!") and more words of warning to daughters ("Be careful!").

Where to Learn More

- Free-Range Kids—the book and the website by Lenore Skenazy (stories of just how out of control our fear has grown)

  www.freerangekids.com/

- "Playing It Safe. Too Safe?"

  www.bamradionetwork.com/educators-channel/756-playing-it-safe-too-safe

- "Risky Play: Why Children Love It and Need It"

  www.psychologytoday.com/blog/freedom-learn/201404/risky-play-why-children-love-it-and-need-it

- "Are We About to Ban Childhood Altogether?"

  www.canberratimes.com.au/younger-kids/kids-education/are-we-about-to-ban-childhood-altogether-20140902-3eqtg.html

(Continued)

(Continued)

- "The Cult of Kiddie Danger"

  http://weeklywonk.newamerica.net/articles/cult-kiddie-danger/

- "Recess Without Rules"

  www.theatlantic.com/education/archive/2014/01/recess-without-rules/283382/

- "Why Rough and Tumble Play Is Really Good"

  www.bamradionetwork.com/parents-channel/282-why-rough-and-tumble-play-is-really-good

CHAPTER 5

When Did a Hug Become a Bad Thing?

There was a time when the conventional wisdom was that we needed four hugs a day to survive, eight hugs a day to maintain, and twelve to grow. Later, as media reports of sexual assault cases spread like viruses, along with fear of lawsuits, educators and children were schooled in "bad touch" versus "good touch" (a hug at that time was still one of the latter). Now, more and more, we have *no* touch.

Sadly, America has always been a low-touch society. Consider that in many other cultures, babies are held for hours, stroked when in need of soothing, and carried close to the bodies of their mothers. In Japan, the closeness between mother and child is so much a part of the culture that there's a word for it: *skinship*. In our culture, babies spend lengthy periods alone in cribs; we fear that unless they're allowed to "self-soothe," they'll be spoiled and grow up dependent. And though we may carry our infants, they're more likely to be "containerized" than carried body-to-body. In fact, on *Good Morning America* a few years ago, a child psychologist lamented the fact that American infants are spending up to *60 waking hours* per week *in* things.

The idea of containerized kids is disturbing for a number of reasons, not the least of which is lack of touch. But when teacher education programs begin advising its students to put up a high-five when a kid requests a hug, and teachers' unions instruct educators to refrain from touching kids at all, as reported in an

Education Week blog, things are getting ridiculous. It's time to take a step back and reassess our priorities.

According to an article on the website of the Council for Exceptional Children, the Pennsylvania State Education Association offers the following guidelines on the use of touch: (1) consider the age, sex, and perception (maturity) of the child, (2) use touch only to praise or comfort, (3) ensure there is another adult present, and (4) briefly touch only the shoulder or arm.

Can't you see it now? A young child (how does that apply to guideline number one?) is crying and desperately in need of comfort (that meets guideline number two). But your aide (if you even have one) is in the media room with some of the other children (number three isn't possible), so you tentatively pat the child on the shoulder (phew, number four applied) and say, "There, there." The child isn't remotely comforted, but you can rest assured that you've followed guidelines and are in no jeopardy of being sued for child abuse.

But isn't *this* child abuse? According to Frances Carlson, author of *Essential Touch: Meeting the Needs of Young Children*, physical contact can be more important to sustaining life than food and water! As she told me in an interview for BAM Radio Network, children need physical contact in order to thrive and grow in every aspect of development. She cited research indicating that when children are denied touch, they fail to grow physically and to develop the emotional and social skills they need to succeed in early childhood and in life.

Dr. Lisa Fiore, Director of Early Childhood Education at Lesley University, who joined Frances and me for the discussion, pointed out that it's not just in school that children aren't getting the touch they need. Our changing society has resulted in "people engaging in activities requiring less physical contact every day."

Truly, when we consider the amount of time children are spending in front of television, telephone, and computer screens, the lack of opportunity for old-fashioned, rough-and-tumble play, and reports of children as old as four and five being pushed in strollers (meaning their hands aren't even being held), we begin to realize just how seldom the child's need for touch is being met.

Ironically, Carlson and Fiore pointed out that when *men* teach young children, the kids are more likely to have their touch needs met because men engage in more physical play than do women. They're also more likely than female teachers to have a hand on the child's back while engaging in conversation. But, sadly, it is the touch from the male teacher that is most suspect of all.

Dr. Fiore concluded our discussion by asking, "Wouldn't it be lovely to embrace touching in the classroom as appropriate and developmentally necessary?"

Wouldn't it be lovely, indeed, if we could put the children's needs ahead of our fears? Even if we discount the research, along with conventional wisdom, we at least should ask ourselves—if we're craving a hug, is a high-five really gonna cut it?

What's a Teacher to Do?

- Carlson recommended that, rather than no-touch policies, schools begin to establish "touch" policies that explain the boundaries of what touch looks like in education settings and that help teachers and parents understand that denying children touch is as problematic as denying access to rest, water, or the bathroom.

- A study by Mary Beth Lawton showed that teachers are more likely to use touch for caretaking or controlling purposes than to comfort, express affection, or play. Pay attention to how you use touch in the classroom, and if you find you're part of the former group, make it a goal to become part of the latter.

- Don't create rules that discourage children from touching one another. For example, requiring a child to ask another if it's okay to give a hug will often discourage the impulse of the hugger and also causes children to think that perhaps such things as hugs are inappropriate. By the same token, you should help children realize that everyone has physical boundaries and that there are cues that will indicate when touch is not wanted.

- Encourage games that involve touching. For example, Musical Hugs invites participants to move in any way they want while the music is playing and to hug the nearest person when the music stops. It Takes Two requires partners to connect such body parts as right hands, left elbows, or opposite feet and to discover how many ways they can move while remaining connected. If you occasionally join the children in these games, you'll have an opportunity to touch and be touched as well.

(Continued)

(Continued)

• Don't discourage rough-and-tumble play among young kids!

• If your school has a no-touch policy, gather as much research as you can and *fight back*. Band together with other teachers and take the research to your administrators and/or school board.

Where to Learn More

• "Touching Children in the Classroom: Why No-Touch Policies Are Harmful"

www.bamradionetwork.com/educators-channel/360-touching-children-in-the-classroom-why-no-touch-policies-harmful

• "Why Rough-and-Tumble Play Is Really Good"

www.bamradionetwork.com/movement-play/331-why-rough-and-tumble-play-is-really-good

• "The Problem with 'No Hug' Policies in School"

http://ideas.time.com/2012/06/19/the-problem-with-no-hug-policies-in-schoo/

CHAPTER 6

Teaching Girls They're More Than a Pretty Face

"Study after study shows that girls believe that how they look is the key to their popularity—that how they look is the key to their self-esteem. Over and over, they think how they look is who they are—how they look is how they feel. And we need them to know that is not true."

These are the words of Peggy Orenstein, author of *Cinderella Ate My Daughter*. She and Diane Levin, coauthor of *So Sexy, So Soon*, had joined me for a discussion on BAM Radio Network. Diane concurred that for girls, appearance determines their value. Worse, they both agreed, a girl's appearance is more often—at younger and younger ages—being defined by how *sexy* she is.

That's a statement that should shock and concern all of us—as should the information that nearly half of *three- to six-year-old* girls now worry about being fat, nearly half of six- to nine-year-old girls wear lipstick or gloss, and that the sexualization of children has led to eating disorders in those as young as six. Children also rank body image among their highest concerns. What were your highest concerns when you were six years old? Mine were having enough time to play and trying to master the cartwheel.

These findings should serve as a wake-up call for all who live and work with children. While it may seem to be an issue of concern to parents only, because children spend much of their time in school and childcare settings, educators must also take notice. They, together with parents, can play an important role in helping young girls grasp that they are more than how they look. And they can start with how they talk to girls.

But that's actually harder than it sounds. Attorney, author, and *Huffington Post* blogger Lisa Bloom has described how challenging it is upon meeting or seeing a little girl to restrain herself from her first impulse, "which is to tell them how darn cute/pretty/beautiful/well-dressed/well-manicured/well-coiffed they are." And, of course, she's not the only one; we all do it. Little girls are just so darn precious that we can't help ourselves. We take one look and squeal, "Don't you look adorable today!" "I love that dress you're wearing!" "Oooh, what a pretty ribbon you've got in your hair!"

So why wouldn't girls believe that their appearance matters first and foremost and that how they look is who they are?

Diane Levin suggested to listeners that, instead, we talk to girls about their interests and abilities. Yes, that may seem like one of those "duh" statements, but just wait until you try it. Like Lisa Bloom, Peggy Orenstein found that it's tough to limit comments about a girl's appearance—that it actually makes adults tense. She admitted that when she first began trying, it felt awkward—as though, by not saying something positive, she was tacitly saying something *negative* about their appearance.

But, awkward as it may be, we need to make the effort. And, yes, it will be challenging in the beginning. First, you won't hear those appearance-related words until *after* they've escaped your lips. But eventually you'll be able to bite them back prior to their escape. And before you know it, talking to girls about a whole host of topics will have become the norm. And this is as it should be.

Now, I imagine there are those who believe that we as a society have far more important things to worry about. But I doubt there's a single person who would disagree that it's completely unacceptable for three- to six-year-olds to be worried about being fat. And six-year-olds wearing lipstick? There's not one reason in the world why a child that age should feel as though she has to enhance her looks by artificial means.

These ideas aren't popping into children's heads on their own. They receive their messages from the adults in their world—in both subtle and not-so-subtle ways. As Diane and Peggy pointed out to me, this is a societal issue, much of it stemming from marketing. And while we may feel overwhelmed at the idea of stopping *that* machine, we have to realize that, child by child, we *can* make a difference.

So head on over to the nearest little girl. Ask for her thoughts on the book she's most recently read, on her favorite sport, or even on the day's weather. Trust me, she'll be happy to tell you what she thinks.

What's a Teacher to Do?

• The occasional comment about appearance is okay. Just watch the ratio. Perhaps every time you pay a compliment without thinking you can balance it with a comment about something of interest to the girl.

• As an educator, you can provide images of females who are known, not for their teeny-tiny size, their gyrations on TV, or their provocative poses on magazine covers but for the work they do, for the admiration they garner through contributions they make to society, and for the thoughts they think!

• Choose books to read in which female characters are strong and capable.

• Take your students on field trips to see female doctors, dentists, chefs, firefighters, and postmasters at work.

• Invite women who are police officers, artists, veterinarians, military personnel, or musicians to visit the classroom. These kinds of activities allow the boys, as well as the girls, to perceive females in a whole new way.

Where to Learn More

- "How We Teach Girls to Have Unhealthy Self-Image"
  www.bamradionetwork.com/educators-channel/673-how-we-teach-girls-to-have-unhealthy-self-image

- "How to Talk to Little Girls"
  www.huffingtonpost.com/lisa-bloom/how-to-talk-to-little-gir_b_882510.html

- Peggy Orenstein's website (www.peggyorenstein.com) offers an ever-evolving list of resources: including picture books, movies, and more to support you in your quest.

- TRUCE (Teachers Resisting Unhealthy Children's Entertainment www.truceteachers.org) offers information and support.

CHAPTER 7

Doing Away With the "Baby Stuff"

When a school chief in Maryland declared that it was time to do away with the "baby stuff" in preschool, he was referring to naptime. My first thoughts were, *When did preschoolers stop being babies in the lifespan of the average human being?* And, *When did scientific findings change with regard to the human need for sleep? I must have missed that research.*

I don't know why the statement surprised me. The pressure for students to spend more time on academics and to pass test after test—to win the race that education has become—is so great that basic human needs are being ignored and unmet. That becomes pretty clear when you learn of the ridiculous policies schools have implemented around even bathroom breaks.

Those are troubling in their own right. But the problem with doing away with naptime for preschoolers *and* kindergartners—with ignoring the need for sleep for students of all ages—is that it's counterintuitive. As experts attest, there are innumerable classroom problems directly traceable to sleep deprivation.

Consider these, mentioned by Dr. James Maas, an international authority on sleep and performance, in a BAM Radio interview:

- Irritability
- Anxiety
- Slowed reaction time
- Reduced ability to process information

- Reduced ability to concentrate
- Reduced ability to remember
- Reduced ability to be creative
- Reduced ability to make critical decisions

One look at that list and anyone responsible for school policy should be able to comprehend that a sleepy student is not a top-performing student. Not even close. In fact, Dr. Maas likened our students to zombies. "Their bodies are there, but their brains are back on their pillows," he said.

Then we add to it what Dr. Mary Sheedy Kurcinka, author of *Sleepless in America*, had to say about behavior problems (the bane of a teacher's existence), and you've got some pretty powerful reasons to ensure that kids get enough sleep.

Dr. Kurcinka contended that "a very significant percentage of challenging behaviors are actually the result of tired kids." In fact, she states that in her practice, 95 percent of the kids presented to her with challenging behaviors are short on sleep.

It makes sense. We've all had days—or weeks—when we were overtired and grumpy. When we'd gladly bite the head off of anyone who looks at us sideways. Why should it be any different for kids, who require even more sleep than we do? Dr. Kurcinka pointed out that if you're tired, you can't manage your emotions. And if you can't manage your own emotions, you can't read those of others. The result is often conflict.

Overtired kids are also wired, clumsy, and unable to focus and pay attention, all of which can result in more negative emotion and behavior—and even accidents.

A kindergartner, she said, still needs twelve hours of sleep a night—and ten to eleven hours for a school-aged child. But because most parents don't know that, they're satisfied with their children getting around eight hours of sleep. Considering that sleep deprivation is cumulative, it's not much of an exaggeration to say that our schools truly are filled with zombies.

Where sleep is concerned, not only do the policymakers fail to understand child development; they also, according to Dr. Maas, don't understand biology.

We talk so much about preparing kids for school but give very little thought to preparing schools for kids. What sense does it make to create a schedule that defies a human body's natural needs and inclinations? Anyone who pushes for earlier start times in schools is clueless. Anyone determined to do away with naptime for our youngest students—who would force them to power through their fatigue, as we adults must so often do—is not only clueless but cruel.

What's a Teacher to Do?

• Two teachers who joined the BAM segment recommended getting to know your students before they enter your classroom on the first day. Examine their permanent records, looking for medical and behavioral issues. Ascertain the reasons why students may be sleepy or perhaps why you might expect them to be sleepy.

• Realize that some kids who are acting out, or who are overactive, are simply trying to stay awake. If that's the case, consider solutions rather than penalties.

• Educate parents about the amount of sleep their kids actually need!

• Educate the students themselves. Even before kids begin to take responsibility for their own sleep—and certainly after they do—they need to understand the reasons why adequate sleep is important, as well as the problems associated with lack of sleep.

• Alert both parents and students to the fact that using electronic devices within an hour of bedtime can result in an inability to fall asleep for thirty to sixty minutes. This is the result of the devices' output of blue-daylight spectrum light, which blocks the flow of melatonin in the brain.

• Alert both parents and students to the fact that children metabolize caffeine much more slowly than do adults. Dr. Kurcinka pointed out that a cola drink at lunch can affect sleep eight to ten hours later.

• Advocate for school policies that take child development—and biology—into consideration. Show them the data that proves how much better students do both academically and athletically when they have adequate sleep.

• If you teach the youngest students, make sure naps or rest time are included in their day—regardless of what anybody says.

Where to Learn More

- "Five Classroom Problems Directly Traceable to Student Sleep Deprivation"

  www.bamradionetwork.com/educators-channel/1061-five-classroom-problems-directly-traceable-to-student-sleep-deprivation

- "What Do Students Need Most? More Sleep"

  http://parenting.blogs.nytimes.com/2014/01/15/what-do-students-need-most-more-sleep/?_php=true&_type=blogs&_r=0

- "Cutting Nap Time May Hurt Preschoolers' Learning, Study Finds"

  http://abcnews.go.com/blogs/health/2013/09/23/cutting-nap-time-may-hurt-preschoolers-learning-study-finds/

CHAPTER 8

"But Competition Is Human Nature"

"It's a dog-eat-dog world out there; children need to learn how to survive in it."

"The earlier children learn that they have to fight for what they want, the better off they'll be."

"It's human nature to want to compete."

I often hear comments such as these when I advocate for cooperation, versus competition, for young children. But, then, the subject of competition is one that provokes strong feelings in the United States. The prevailing belief is that competition is good for us, that someone without a strong, competitive nature is just a wimp, and that to be non-competitive is to have been born without a necessary gene. And the push for competition is only growing stronger in this country. How else to explain such trends as children barely out of diapers being enrolled in soccer training programs and the birth of television shows such as *Toddlers & Tiaras* and *Dance Moms*?

Is competition really human nature? Does it serve children better to learn to compete than to cooperate? Is the "real world" truly a place that requires us to prepare our children to battle, rather than belong, to clash, rather than collaborate, and to see everyone else as foe, not friend?

In an essay in the *New York Times* several years ago, Nicholas Kristof answered the first question for me when he told the story of his attempts to teach the game of musical chairs to a group of five-year-old Japanese children. His efforts proved unsuccessful—because the children kept politely stepping out of the way so their peers could sit in the chairs! Sounds just like American kids, right?

This certainly seems to indicate that "dog-eat-dog" behavior is taught in some societies and not in others. Indeed, the contention that being competitive is learned behavior, and more cultural than natural, is supported by a number of experts in the social sciences. Conversely, the belief that competition is human nature isn't supported by research; it's simply one of those things we've spouted so often that it's become an urban legend.

Is there competition in life? Sure. But I don't believe it's as wide-ranging as is commonly proclaimed.

For example, it's not as though there are only six A's allotted per classroom. If kids want to do well in school they have to work for it—not in a way that causes someone else to fail but by doing their own personal best. If they want to get into a good college, it's the same thing. Yes, there are only so many placements at each university, but if they've put forth the appropriate effort, learned a good work ethic, and are people with character, regardless of whether they get into their first or third choice of schools, they're going to be just fine.

The same pertains when they apply for the job of their dreams. Yes, they're competing against other applicants, but it's unlikely they even know who those other applicants are and what they bring to the table. Nor can they be aware of all the factors involved in the selection process. All they can do in that situation, once again, is to be their own personal best.

In answer to the questions about children being better served by learning to compete, it's important to consider that when children are consistently placed in situations where winning is the ultimate goal—where the winners are considered heroes and the losers "losers"—winning is what children come to value. They learn that only the end result (the win) counts—not the process (the effort) involved in getting there. This means that extrinsic reward is granted more validity than intrinsic reward. And while that may not seem like such a bad thing in a goal-oriented society, we have to remember the young child's stage of development. Children under the age of 8 are motivated by pleasure. Winning feels good when everyone around you is offering congratulations, but the kudos don't last, so the good feelings don't either. And what about the children who aren't winning?

On the other hand, when children are given the chance to *cooperate*—to work together toward a solution or common goal, whether cowriting a story or finding a way to fit inside a single plastic hoop, the experience feels good from the inside out. Often, the sound of laughter reigns. Each child realizes she or he plays a vital role in the outcome, contributing to the success of the venture, and each accepts the responsibility of fulfilling that role. Participants also learn to become tolerant of others' ideas and to accept the similarities and differences of others. Furthermore, cooperative activities seldom cause the feelings of inferiority that can result from the comparisons made during competition. On the contrary, because cooperative and noncompetitive activities lead to greater chances for success, they generate more confidence in children.

Alfie Kohn's *No Contest: The Case Against Competition* is perhaps the quintessential book on this topic. In it, he has identified much research demonstrating the positive effects of cooperation on social and emotional development. He contends that cooperation

- is more conducive to emotional health;
- leads to friendlier feelings among participants;
- promotes a feeling of being in control of one's life;
- increases self-esteem;
- results in greater sensitivity and trust toward others; and
- increases motivation.

I'll concede that there are occasions in life when we must compete. But if we consider the number of relationships in our lives—familial, spousal, work- and community-related—we have to admit that there are more opportunities for cooperation and collaboration than competition.

Still think teaching children to compete is more important and that it's wimpy to go against "human nature?" Well, all I can say is that a 2013 article in *Forbes* identified the top ten qualities employers are seeking in twenty-something employees and the number-one quality was the ability to work in a team.

Which leads us to perhaps the most important question in this piece: where are today's children going to learn such a thing?

What's a Teacher to Do?

• Educators are in a unique position to truly prepare children to become a part of society and to succeed in tomorrow's "real world." You can—and should—share information with parents regarding the detriments of competition and the benefits of cooperation. Tell them about the *Forbes* article; they all want their kids to make a positive impression in their future employment.

• Read and assign stories and books involving cooperation.

• Don't hold contests or assign gold stars or stickers to the "best" students.

• Offset society's propensity for competition by focusing specifically on cooperation. Play and facilitate *cooperative* games instead of those that eliminate and discriminate. Challenge the children to find ways to create geometric shapes with partners and groups, to create partner and group balances, and to work together to solve movement and academic problems, such as using their hands to measure one another's height or using their bodies to form the shape of letters or numbers. Ask pairs of children to keep a balloon in the air, taking turns tapping it and counting the number of times they touch it within a predetermined time frame. How many children does it take to blow a feather across the floor?

• Offer opportunities for pairs and groups of students to participate in collaborative learning. Arrange your classroom to allow for it.

Where to Learn More

- "Creating a Non-Competitive Climate for Children" with Alfie Kohn

  www.bamradionetwork.com/educators-channel/158-creating-a-non-competitive-climate-for-children

- "The Case Against Competition" by Alfie Kohn

  www.alfiekohn.org/parenting/tcac.htm

- "Setting Up Your Classroom to Maximize Collaborative Learning"

  www.bamradionetwork.com/educators-channel/2140-setting-up-your-classroom-to-support-collaborative-learning

- "Why Working Toward a Common Goal Is More Important Than Getting an 'A'"

  www.bamradionetwork.com/educators-channel/2152-working-toward-a-common-goal-more-important-than-working-toward-an-qaq

- *Cooperative Games and Sports: Joyful Activities for Everyone* by Terry Orlick

- *Great Games for Young Children: Over 100 Games to Develop Self-Confidence, Problem-Solving Skills, and Cooperation* by Rae Pica

CHAPTER 9

Terrorist Tots?

In the wake of the Sandy Hook school shooting and other such incidents, school safety is understandably a concern. But does school safety necessitate actions like the following?

- Two six-year-old boys in Maryland were suspended while playing cops and robbers during recess and using their fingers to make imaginary guns.
- Also in Maryland, another six-year-old was suspended for making a gun gesture with his finger, pointing at a classmate and saying "pow."
- A five-year-old in rural Pennsylvania was suspended from kindergarten after telling another girl that she was going to shoot her with her pink Hello Kitty toy gun that discharges bubbles. School officials labeled the child a "terrorist threat" and interrogated her for three hours without her parents present (what were they *thinking*?).

If you're wondering what these stories have to do with curbing school violence, I'm with you. But many readers likely are in favor of such zero tolerance efforts; they don't view these incidents as overreactions. After all, the thinking goes, if we stop such behaviors at a young age, children, schools, and the world in general will be a much safer place.

That may be the conventional wisdom—but that doesn't necessarily make it true. What's more likely is that these children and others like them, who are scolded, shamed, and suspended merely for doing what children *do*, will now feel anxious, powerless, and vulnerable. And that can't be good for anybody.

Just ask the experts. I did—on two separate occasions. In the first discussion, with Gerard Jones and Nancy Carlsson-Paige, I posed questions about war, gun, and superhero play. Does it demonstrate a tendency for violence? Should it be prohibited? The answer, even from Carlsson-Paige, a child development expert celebrated for her work in peace education, was a resounding *no*.

Jones, the author of *Killing Monsters: Why Children Need Fantasy, Super Heroes, and Make-Believe Violence*, and Carlsson-Paige, author of *The War Play Dilemma: What Every Parent and Teacher Needs to Know*, were adamant that children require this kind of fantasy play (*fantasy* being the key word). They need it to make sense of the world around them, to learn to differentiate between fiction and reality, and to work out their fears. When young children see something scary in the media (and they see more than we think they do), it's through their play that they explore and express their feelings about it.

Still, many educators, parents, and school administrators seem unaware of this. It was with dismay that I read a conversation on Facebook in which one early childhood professional after another proudly proclaimed she had implemented a zero tolerance policy around "violence." No cops and robbers. No superheroes. No "bang-bang" with guns made out of fingers, carrots, sticks, or any other implement in a child's arsenal.

Certainly, these professionals are well-intentioned. But as Gerard Jones told me, when we bring too much of our adult anxiety to children, we make them fretful about their fantasy and play. Instead of enabling them to understand that fantasy is safe because it's not real, we force children to think about the reality of what they're playing at. We impose our adult anxieties about real guns and real violence on them. It's in the classroom, he insisted, that we need to *encourage* children to "play these things out," to build fantasies, and to work their concerns and fears into an imaginary life.

Carlsson-Paige expressed concern about children who don't get opportunities for this kind of play. "Where does it go inside of them?" she asked. "How does it affect them?"

As both of these experts attested, a zero tolerance policy is problematic. Not having one, on the other hand, doesn't mean that anything goes. There is a middle ground, and educators and childcare professionals are in the best position to understand this and to help children find it.

Looking beyond the short-term, Carlsson-Paige says,

> We really have to shift our thinking about how we're handling the question of violence with young people. It's a matter of long-term prevention of violence and not a punitive-discipline, one-event response to an act that we see. . . . [H]ow do we create a climate where children feel safe, where they learn to care about other people, where they learn to respect differences and skills for resolving conflict, and all of these things that provide the background for a non-violent person and a non-violent society? It's a long-term solution we have to reach for, and right now we're at the opposite end of doing that with this quick-response-to-an-event kind of approach.

I concur—and I fervently hope that with the necessary understanding and information, adults will stop making children feel like terrorists when they're simply behaving like children.

What's a Teacher to Do?

There *are* alternatives to the outright banning of gun and superhero play. Carlsson-Paige makes the following recommendations:

• Put boundaries around the play, perhaps having it occur in a contained space; for example, only outside or in a certain area of the playground.

• Don't allow children to bring in fabricated war toys, but do let them make some of their own guns and swords with open-ended materials.

• Help children expand their stories beyond imitation of what they see on TV or in movies.

• Use all of your child development knowledge to appreciate the things children are doing. To look at their play and ask yourself what issues you see coming up for the kids as they're playing. Does the play look safe? Does it look like they're working out their fears in a creative way, or are they stuck in a violent scenario?

Where to Learn More

- "War, Gun, and Super Hero Play. Good or Bad?"

  www.bamradionetwork.com/educators-channel/496-war-gun-and-super-hero-play-good-or-bad

- "Children Playing with Toy Guns and Imaginary Assault Weapons in School. Problem?"

  www.bamradionetwork.com/educators-channel/983-children-playing-with-toy-guns-and-imaginary-assault-weapons-in-school-problem

- "What's a Teacher to Do?: Superhero Play; Television and Children's Play"

  www.turben.com/article/83/582/What%92s-a-Teacher-to-Do%3F—Superhero-Play%3A-Television-and-Children%92s-Play%3B-Aggressive-Play

- *Under Deadman's Skin: Discovering the Meaning of Children's Violent Play* by Jane Katch

PART II

Understanding the Mind/Body Connection

CHAPTER 10

The Myth of the Brain/Body Dichotomy

As you'd expect, when the Texas State School Board was voting whether or not to make daily physical education part of the curriculum, there was a lot of deliberation. Naturally, time and money are always at issue where a subject such as physical education (PE) is concerned. But in the case of this particular content area, there is another factor that creates debate: the myth of the brain/body dichotomy. It is precisely this myth that caused one board member to pronounce, "If we have daily PE the kids will be healthy but dumb!"

Such is the legacy of philosopher Rene Descarte, whose declaration, "I think, therefore I am," was the beginning of mind/body dualism—the belief that the mind and body are separate entities. If it hadn't had such an adverse effect on the lives and education of our children throughout the ages, I might find the concept and its acceptance fascinating. But rather than fascinate, it infuriates me. I've been beating my head against this particular wall for more than 30 years—and I'm stymied as to why such a belief ever caught on, let alone why it has lasted as long as it has.

Granted, they didn't have the research during Descarte's time that we have today. But anyone who has ever taken a walk that sparked insight or an idea should be able to make the connection— as should anyone who finds himself thinking more clearly while pacing than while sitting or immediately following a run. And they surely had plenty of research that they could have referenced as they debated in Texas.

So why are we still behaving as if children consist of heads only? Or is it just that we wish they did?

In his book, *Teaching Children Physical Education*, George Graham describes his experiences going before school boards and administrators to convince them to add or return PE to the curriculum. He tells them it would be great—and, in fact, very cost-efficient—if we could just bus the children's *heads* to school. But, gee, those heads don't come unaccompanied.

Also in Graham's book is a cartoon depicting headless children entering the gym. The moral? Children must not move in the classroom or think in the gym—because, after all, the brain and body supposedly have nothing to do with one another.

But consider the following:

- Numerous studies have demonstrated that physically active students perform better in, and have better attitudes toward, school.
- Movement is the young child's preferred—and most effective—mode of learning, but we make them sit still regardless. Why do we insist on teaching children in any way other than via their preferred—and *most effective*—method?
- Numerous studies suggest that because the child's earliest learning is based on motor development so, too, is subsequent knowledge. In a BAM interview, neurophysiologist Carla Hannaford explained, "If you look at brain development, it's very, very clear that all of the areas of the brain are connected to the movement area. The very first areas of the brain are all directly around movement."

Still, physical education and recess (and play in the early childhood classroom) are going the way of the dinosaurs. This sad fact is the direct result not only of mind/body dualism but also of the belief that the functions of the mind are superior to those of the body.

Imagine all of the lost potential through the years as children have been forced to learn in ways that aren't developmentally appropriate for them and that even make them miserable.

Now, on the flip side, envision schools that recognize the mind/body connection. Imagine the enjoyment—for both students and teachers—of a classroom in which few struggle, and everyone looks forward to being there. Imagine a lower dropout rate. Imagine more students completing school with a belief in their ability to succeed.

There are many, many arguments I could make to support the contention that the mind and body are dependent upon one another. But I'll let you read and hear some of them for yourself in the resources listed below—from people far smarter than I.

Instead, I'll end with a couple of quotations:

> We have spent years and resources struggling to teach people to learn and yet the standardized test scores go down and illiteracy rises. Could it be that one of the key elements we've been missing is simply movement?

> I lay it down as an educational axiom that in teaching you will come to grief as soon as you forget that your pupils have bodies.

The first quotation is from Carla Hannaford, a scientist and educator who has been studying the brain/body connection for decades. When she says it, I believe it.

Alfred North Whitehead penned the second sentiment in his book *The Aims of Education and Other Essays*. It pains me to know that those words were written in 1929—and that more than eight decades later, they're still being ignored.

What's a Teacher to Do?

- If you haven't already, read Carla Hannaford's *Smart Moves: Why Learning Is Not All in Your Head*. It's the best—and most accessible—book I've read on the connection between the mind and the body. Share it with fellow teachers and with administrators and school board members. If you have schoolwide or faculty book clubs, make sure it's on the list. Recommend it to parents.

- Regardless of what anybody else believes, embrace the mind/body connection yourself! Add "brain breaks" to your day by occasionally inviting students to stand and jog in place or to do the Cross Crawl, alternating opposite elbow to knee. Lead them in other activities that cross the body's midline (it promotes communication of the brain's hemispheres across the corpus callosum). Allow them to take a quick jaunt around the room. Play a quick game of Simon Says (without the elimination process). These kinds of activities change the chemistry of the brain, boosting norepinephrine and dopamine—the latter of which increases working memory.

• Allow students to stretch or stand as needed.

• Employ active learning in your classroom (see "In Defense of Active Learning").

• Fight for the inclusion—or retention—of physical education and recess in your school (see "Reading, Writing, 'Rithmetic . . . and Recess" and "Why Kids Need 'Gym'").

Where to Learn More

• "Understanding the Child's Mind/Body Connection"
www.bamradionetwork.com/educators-channel/159-understanding-the-childs-mind-body-connection

• "Is the Body the Next Breakthrough in Education Tech?"
http://hechingerreport.org/content/body-next-breakthrough-education-tech_16629/#.U770KQWz03U.twitter

• "Need a Brain Boost? Exercise"
www.washingtonpost.com/lifestyle/wellness/need-a-brain-boost-exercise/2014/05/27/551773f4-db92-11e3-8009-71de85b9c527_story.html

• "Can Exercise Close the Achievement Gap?"
www.psmag.com/navigation/health-and-behavior/can-exercise-close-achievement-gap-83433/#.U6BRDsGCOAc.twitter

• *Spark: The Revolutionary New Science of Exercise and the Brain* by John Ratey, MD

• *Learning With the Body in Mind: The Scientific Basis for Energizers, Movement, Games, and Physical Education* by Eric Jensen

CHAPTER 11

Why Does Sitting Still Equal Learning?

A few years back, Christy Isbell, a pediatric occupational therapist and friend, presented a workshop at the annual conference of the National Association for the Education of Young Children (NAEYC), with a title indicating that the workshop was about teaching children who won't sit still. The exact name escapes me now, but I very clearly recall that more than 2,000 early childhood professionals crammed themselves into the room to listen to her.

I was envious—because my session, about movement, didn't draw half that many! And I joked with Christy that perhaps I'd "borrow" the title and use it for all of my future presentations.

If you think about it, though, it's actually sad that such a title or topic would bring educators out in droves. *Naturally* they were teaching children who won't sit still; they were working with young kids! And so, naturally, they shouldn't have been *trying* to get the kids to stay in one place.

Whether we're talking about preschool, elementary through secondary school, college, or even adult learners, I have serious objections to the idea that learning supposedly only comes via the eyes, the ears, and the seat of the pants. Schools—and policymakers—have for too long accepted the belief that learning best occurs while students are seated (and quiet, of course). The theory may have been understandable back when they didn't have the research to prove otherwise. But today we do.

Today we have research showing that the more senses used in the learning process the higher the percentage of retention. Yet schools still pump data through the eyes, ears, and bottom and expect students to retain it anyway.

Today we have research showing that the brain is far more active during physical activity than while one is seated. Brain-based learning expert Eric Jensen has told me, "The brain is constantly responding to environmental input. Compared to a baseline of sitting in a chair, walking, moving and active learning bumps up blood flow and key chemicals for focus and long-term memory (norepinephrine) as well as for effort and mood (dopamine)." Yet schools and policymakers cling to the belief that the body has nothing to do with how the brain functions.

Today—and this is the big one, from my perspective—we have research demonstrating that sitting in a chair *increases fatigue* and *reduces concentration* (our bodies are designed to move, not sit). Yet policymakers and schools implement policies (more testing; no recess; even fewer bathroom breaks) that require students to do more sitting. What sense can that possibly make?

All of us have had days where we were forced to sit at conferences or meetings—or perhaps on a plane—for endless minutes and hours at a time and found ourselves exhausted at the end of those days. It was perplexing, as all we had done was sit. But, given the research, it's completely understandable.

Eric Jensen has written extensively about this issue. He confirms that the human body isn't made for sitting and that sitting for more than ten minutes at a time reduces our awareness of physical and emotional sensations. Also, the pressure on spinal discs is 30 percent greater while sitting than while standing. None of this contributes to optimal learning.

In truth, it doesn't contribute to optimal health either. Recently there's been a good deal of attention given to new research revealing the many health risks associated with prolonged sitting. It turns out that even if you exercise faithfully, if you spend most of your time sitting you're at risk for heart disease, disability, diabetes, cancer, and obesity, the latter of which brings its own host of health problems. The reports scared the heck out of me, so I've been jumping up from my desk as often as possible each day. No more rolling the office chair over to the printer. No more taking phone calls while seated.

In a BAM Radio segment on the subject of sitting in the classroom, Christy Isbell proclaimed,

> Who's to say we have to sit down to learn? Why can't we stand to learn? Why can't we lay on the floor on our tummies to learn? Why can't we sit in the rocking chair to learn? There are lots of other simple movement strategies. Just changing the position can make a big difference.

Indeed!

Fortunately there are teachers—and even some schools—bucking the system and allowing students to sit on exercise balls or to work at tables or standing desks.

In one study, researchers equipped four first-grade classrooms in Texas with standing desks. What they found was that, even though the desks were equipped with stools of the appropriate height for sitting, 70 percent of the students never used their stools, and the other 30 percent stood the majority of the time. Moreover, the researchers discovered that standing increased attention, alertness, engagement, and on-task behavior among the students—a dream come true for any teacher!

Recently I tweeted the image of two brain scans published by the University of Illinois' Dr. Chuck Hillman. One scan showed the brain after sitting quietly and the other following a 20-minute walk. The difference was remarkable, with the latter *far* more "lit up" than the former. I think it's a great sign that the tweet received dozens of retweets and "favorites" and that, to this day, it's still being shared. And I absolutely adored the response of teacher Dee Kalman, who said the images offered scientific proof for her teaching mantra: "When the bum is numb, the mind is dumb."

I couldn't have said it better myself.

What's a Teacher to Do?

- Offer brain breaks such as those suggested in "The Myth of the Brain/BodyDichotomy." Neurophysiologist Carla Hannaford, in the same interview with Christy Isbell, suggested that teachers let students know *why* they're being asked to move occasionally. She said they need to know that they're activating whole-brain function, and it will make their learning easier. She also recommended that the students themselves lead the brain breaks.

- When possible, use the design of your classroom to reduce time spent sitting. Designs with various learning centers, or those that promote collaborative learning among ever-changing partners and groups, offer opportunities for the students to move more frequently.

- Take advantage of professional development opportunities to learn more about incorporating brain breaks and using movement across the curriculum.

Where to Learn More

- "Teaching Children Who Just Won't Sit Still"

  www.bamradionetwork.com/educators-channel/326-teaching-strategieshandling-young-students-who-just-wont-sit-still

- "Moving with the Brain in Mind" by Eric Jensen (a must-read)

  www.nemours.org/content/dam/nemours/www/filebox/service/preventive/nhps/pep/braininmind.pdf

- *Energizers! 88 Quick Movement Activities That Refresh and Refocus, K–6* by Susan Lattanzi Roser

CHAPTER 12

In Defense of Active Learning

In the past, based on what they knew about and observed in young children, teachers designed their programs to meet their students' developmental needs. Play and active learning were considered key tools to accommodate those needs and to facilitate children's education. Typical activities in the earliest grades included

- sorting and stacking blocks and other manipulatives (providing mathematical knowledge);
- singing and dancing, or acting out stories (emergent literacy);
- growing plants from seeds, exploring the outdoor environment, and investigating at sand and water tables (scientific knowledge); and
- trying on various roles and interacting with one another at housekeeping and other dramatic-play centers (social studies).

Today, these types of lessons are steadily disappearing. Due to an increasing emphasis on "academics" and accountability, policymakers are demanding more and more testing, which requires more and more seatwork. Indeed, one refrain I hear from teachers more than any other is, "We don't have time for movement [play] anymore; we're too busy working on academics [meeting standards; fill in the blank]."

It may no longer be acceptable to run, jump, and dance in the early childhood classroom simply for the joy and the physical, social, and emotional benefits of it (sad but true), but what if movement has cognitive benefits? What if it can be used to help children meet standards?

Consider the following: When children move over, under, around, through, beside, and near objects and others, they better grasp the meaning of these prepositions and geometry concepts. When they perform a "slow walk" or skip "lightly," adjectives and adverbs become much more than abstract ideas. When they're given the opportunity to physically demonstrate such action words as *stomp, pounce, stalk,* or *slither*—or descriptive words such as *smooth, strong, gentle,* or *enormous*—word comprehension is immediate and long-lasting. The words are in context, as opposed to being a mere collection of letters. This is what promotes emergent literacy and a love of language.

Similarly, if children take on high, low, wide, and narrow body shapes, they'll have a much greater understanding of these quantitative concepts—and opposites—than do children who are merely presented with the words and their definitions. When they act out the lyrics to "Roll Over" ("There were five in the bed and the little one said, 'roll over'"), they can see that five minus one leaves four. The same understanding—and fascination—results when children have personal experience with such scientific concepts as gravity, flotation, evaporation, magnetics, balance and stability, and action and reaction.

The following are two stories I've come across that help illustrate the significance of active learning. The first is of a preschool teacher who conducted a mock class with parents, in which the lesson was to learn about kiwi fruit. Half of the parents were told about kiwis and then given a coloring sheet, along with brown and green crayons. The other half took a "field trip" to the tree in the hall, where they were able to smell, feel, and taste the fruit. Not surprisingly, the latter group of parents left with a much greater understanding of kiwis. And those were adults who, unlike young children, are well beyond the stage of concrete thinking.

The second story is that of a fifth grader who had numerous creative movement experiences outside of school. One day, as his teacher was trying to help her class understand the workings of the human heart via the textbooks open on their desks, this boy raised his hand and asked if they could "do it." His teacher was puzzled but allowed him to continue, at which point he arranged the children so that some were the arteries opening and closing and others the blood flowing through. Voila! The students understood how the human heart works!

Both of these stories also serve to illustrate that it is not only in early childhood education that active learning has significant benefits.

Noted educator and author Eric Jensen labels the learning described above as *implicit*—such as learning to ride a bike. At the other end of the continuum is *explicit* learning—such as being told the capital of Peru. He asks, If you hadn't ridden a bike in five years, would you still be able to do it? And, If you hadn't heard the capital of Peru for five years, would you still remember what it was? Explicit learning may get the facts across more quickly than learning through exploration and discovery, but the latter has far more meaning to children and stays with them longer.

In a discussion I facilitated for BAM Radio, neurophysiologist Carla Hannaford stated that we learn 80 percent of what we experience physically and sensorially but only 10 percent of what we read.

She also contends, "If we didn't move, we wouldn't need a brain."

And, oh, there's one last point I'd like to make in defense of active learning. Movement is the young child's preferred mode of learning. Why would we want to teach them in any way that isn't their preference?

What's a Teacher to Do?

• Whenever possible, give your students the opportunity to physically experience concepts, as in the examples given here. If your students are learning to count, ask them to place a certain number of body parts on the floor. If you want to work on simple computation, after placing the designated number of body parts on the floor, ask them to subtract one part. How many are left? To help them distinguish between a lowercase "b" and a lowercase "d," invite them to take partners and together create first one and then the other. Whatever the content area, there are ways to physically experience its concepts.

• Keep Gardner's theory of multiple intelligences in mind when facilitating learning. Do your students need to act out a concept (bodily-kinesthetic intelligence), make up a song about it (musical intelligence), draw a picture of it (visual intelligence), and so forth?

• I once heard a story about a school in which kindergarten teachers who permitted movement and play in the classroom were reprimanded by their administration. It's my sincere hope that this is an extreme example, but I suspect it may not be. Should you find yourself in a similar situation the first step, as always, is to gather together the research, of which there is more and more, on the body's role in learning, and take it to your administrators. You can start with the resources below.

Where to Learn More

• "Recognizing and Nurturing the Intelligence of Movement" www.bamradionetwork.com/educators-channel/394-identi fying-nurturing-the-intelligence-of-movement

• "Making Stories Come Alive" by Annie Murphy Paul http://anniemurphypaul.com/2014/04/making-stories-come-alive/

• "Bringing the Body to Digital Learning" by Annie Murphy Paul http://anniemurphypaul.com/2014/07/bringing-the-body-to-digital-learning/

• *Smart Moves: Why Learning Is Not All in Your Head* by Carla Hannaford

• *Spark: The Revolutionary New Science of Exercise and the Brain* by John Ratey

• My books *Jump into Literacy, Jump into Math,* and *Jump into Science*

CHAPTER 13

"Play" Is Not a Four-Letter Word

Recreation and leisure, to my knowledge, have never held a high value in the United States. Instead, we value hard work, achievement, and accomplishment. All are worthy of our respect and pride. But isn't it ironic that a country whose constitution allows for the pursuit of happiness seems to feel a collective guilt about the very idea of anything fun? And it's getting worse all the time. "Busy" is the new status symbol. "Overwhelmed" is the new normal, as a colleague of mine likes to say.

How did this happen? When did productivity and busyness become our number-one priorities? Even given the Puritan work ethic, life in the States has become so unbalanced that one side of the seesaw is pretty much grounded.

If that's how adults choose to live, fine; they're able to make their own choices. But why must we insist that children, who by their very nature are playful, share these particular values? Why are we so eager for our children to "act like adults?" Especially considering that adults can't exactly be called happy or content these days. Far too many are fried from the effects of living a too-full life. So why would we want children to be subjected to anything remotely like that? Having experienced the many negative effects of trying to do too much in too little time—of living lives that are contrary to human nature—why aren't we adults doing everything in our power to *protect* children from a similar fate? Now more than ever, why aren't we doing all we can to ensure children experience true childhood while they have the chance?

Instead, I hear from educators all across the country that children actually don't know how to play anymore. Children! These are creatures *born* to play (just as kittens and puppies are born to play), but because they're so busy being scheduled and supervised and "schooled"—all of which are considered more essential than something as "frivolous" as play—children are losing the knack to do what comes naturally to them. Can you imagine trying to keep kittens and puppies from frolicking, when that is so clearly what nature intended?

In *Keeping Your Kids Out Front Without Kicking Them from Behind*, authors Ian Tofler and Theresa Foy DeGeronimo bluntly write:

> In the process of trying to prepare our children for a rapidly evolving and fiercely competitive world, we too often professionalize and adultify our children by taking the fun out of childhood. We have turned summer camps into training camps where kids work hard to learn and improve useful skills. We have stolen lazy Saturday afternoons spent daydreaming under a tree and replaced them with adult-supervised, adult-organized activities and classes. We have taken kids out of the neighborhood playgrounds and placed them in dance and music classes, in SAT preparation classes, and on organized athletic teams. There is no time that can be wasted on idle pastimes.

Why do we now insist that *accomplishment* and *achievement* be words associated with childhood? *Play* is the word that is supposed to be associated with childhood. And true play is nothing like what Tofler and DeGeronimo describe. True play is open-ended and intrinsically motivated. True play is not directed by adults. It has nothing to do with product (home runs, goals, points, and wins) and everything to do with process (fun).

But true play is being pushed out of children's lives at an alarming rate. If it doesn't serve some "purpose"—like winning a sports trophy or creating a potential Olympian—today's parents have little regard for it. They are part of a culture that has come to see little value in fun.

It pains me to have to reiterate the many benefits children accrue by playing—because that seems to reinforce the demands of those who insist there be "results" from everything children do. I mean, I shouldn't have to defend play for children any more than I should have to defend their eating, sleeping, and breathing.

But it bears emphasizing that the adult personality is built on the child's play. Among the social skills learned are the ability to share, cooperate, negotiate, compromise, make and revise rules, and to take the perspectives of others. Play provides opportunities for children to meet and solve problems—the number-one ability they will most assuredly require in this rapidly changing world. It helps children express their thoughts and feelings and to deal with stress. To cope with fears they can't yet understand or articulate. Through play, children acquire literacy, mathematical, and creative skills. Make-believe play, in particular, has been linked to self-regulation skills, which in turn have been linked to greater academic success than IQ has. Self-regulation skills also help children with self-control and with managing stress while learning. Moreover, if children don't learn to play as *children*, they aren't likely to discover its value as adults. And just think about what a dreary, deadening existence daily life will become without a playful attitude.

Stuart Brown, MD, founder of the National Institute for Play, and psychologist and play researcher Dr. Peter Gray are among the experts who link play deprivation with hostility and depression among children, youths, and adults. They point out that as opportunities for children to play have lessened, aggression and depression have increased. There is no way that's a coincidence.

Really, we have to ask ourselves: If children begin living like adults in childhood, what will there be left to look forward to? And what joy will they find as adults if striving to "succeed" has become life's sole purpose? To my way of thinking, a life without joy can't be considered a successful one.

What's a Teacher to Do?

- If you're a preschool or kindergarten teacher, be sure that your curriculum is play based. Even acquiring knowledge about "academics" can—and should—be achieved through play. Sorting and stacking blocks, for example, is both mathematics and science. Doing it with another child brings in social studies—and, if they're communicating about what they're doing, emergent literacy.

- If you're an early childhood educator being pressured by parents to have a more academics-oriented curriculum, educate them. Help them to understand the value of play. Also, reassure them that their children will not fall behind. Studies have shown that there are neither short-term nor long-term advantages of early academics versus play and that there are no distinguishable differences by first grade. The only difference was that the children who had experienced early academics were more anxious and less creative than their peers who had been in traditional, play-based early childhood programs—a distinctive *dis*advantage.

- If you're being pressured by administrators to have a more academics-oriented curriculum, educate them too. Join with other like-minded teachers and show your administrators the research. Someone with wisdom and knowledge has to stand for the children!

- If you're a teacher in the primary grades, find as many ways as possible to incorporate play and creativity into the curriculum. Use project-based approaches that allow for a certain level of freedom and experimentation. Take brain breaks during which the kids are able to sing or dance. Allow them to act out the plots of stories or to hold mock debates. Incorporate divergent problem solving so kids get to "play" with a variety of responses to challenges.

- Never withhold recess as punishment. Recess may be the only time during which a child has the opportunity to experience free play.

Where to Learn More

- "The Decline of Play," a TEDx Talk with Dr. Peter Gray (a must watch!)

  www.youtube.com/watch?v=Bg-GEzM7iTk

- "The Critical Need for Fantasy Play" with Vivian Gussin-Paley

  www.bamradionetwork.com/educators-channel/52-the-critical-need-for-fantasy-play

- "Why Children Need Different Types of Play" with Stuart Brown

  www.bamradionetwork.com/educators-channel/157-why-children-need-different-types-of-play

- Alliance for Childhood

  www.allianceforchildhood.org

- National Institute for Play

  www.nifplay.org

- American Association for the Child's Right to Play

  www.ipausa.org

CHAPTER 14

The Body Matters, Too

S hould the physical fitness of children be the concern of education professionals? Should teachers have to worry about their students' movement skills, in addition to literacy and numeracy skills? Is it their responsibility to foster their students' health? Or is all of that a matter for the family and the family alone to worry about?

Consider this:

- Forty percent of today's five- to eight-year-olds show at least one heart disease risk factor including hypertension and obesity, the latter of which is rising at faster rates among children than among adults. Should we be saying the words *five-year-old* and *hypertension* in the same sentence?
- The first signs of arteriosclerosis (hardening of the arteries) are now appearing at age five. Ditto the above.
- The Centers for Disease Control and Prevention (CDC) estimates that American children born in the year 2000 face a one-in-three chance of developing type 2 diabetes, previously known as adult-onset diabetes because it was rarely before seen in children. It's become so common now that they had to change the name.
- Children six to ten years old are dying of sudden cardiopulmonary arrest. Remember when people were in their "old age" before this sort of thing happened?
- This may be the first generation of children to have a shorter life span than their parents.

Given these alarming facts and others resulting from the childhood obesity crisis we hear so much about, it seems to me that the state of children's health is the responsibility of all who live and work with kids.

Still, I know it will take more than scary statistics to get everyone to agree with that sentiment. I've stood in front of educators and explained that just as reading and writing skills must be taught in early childhood so, too, must motor skills be taught. I've implored teachers to consider the state of their students' bodies, as well as the state of their minds. I've urged (cajoled?) teachers to take seriously the concept of the whole—thinking, feeling, moving—child. And I've watched many of their faces go blank. I even imagine I can read their thoughts:

I've already got so much to do! Now I have to worry about movement skills and physical fitness, too?

They're just motor skills. It's not as though we're talking about something important, *like language skills.*

But I don't know anything about movement or physical fitness; it wasn't part of my preservice training.

I get it. I really do. How do you fit one more thing into the curriculum? How do you teach something with which you feel wholly unfamiliar and sometimes even uncomfortable? And why bother anyway?

To answer the latter question in the simplest of terms: because physical activity

- reduces the risk of dying prematurely;
- reduces the risk of dying from heart disease;
- reduces the risk of developing diabetes;
- reduces the risk of developing colon cancer;
- reduces feelings of depression and anxiety;
- helps control weight;
- increases the body's infection-fighting white blood cells and germ-fighting antibodies; and
- helps build and maintain healthy bones, muscles, and joints.

And those are just *some* of its benefits.

I strongly believe that as educators, we are responsible for the *whole child*. And it frustrates me that the functions of the mind are considered far superior to those of the body.

I once conducted a staff development workshop with a group of New England elementary school educators in the dead of winter. I did a cartoon double take when told that the kids hadn't had a physically active recess in three weeks because there was too much snow on the playground and no space indoors to accommodate it. Most troubling was my impression that if it weren't for the fact that these restless students were getting on everyone's nerves, the teachers wouldn't have been at all concerned that their students' bodies were being neglected.

Yes, family plays a critical role in fostering children's health and fitness—and in establishing the early habits that lead to wellness. But it's unlikely that, beyond providing space, time, and opportunity for movement, parents will know what to do to promote skill development. Besides, kids spend more time in school settings than they do at home. If schools aren't devoted to children's health—to taking care of their bodies, as well as their brains—then I fear for the future. Not only can we expect all of the sedentary behavior currently supported (and very nearly celebrated) to impact children's futures in very personal ways; also, we will suffer as a society. It's estimated that if current trends continue, by 2030 the medical costs associated with treating preventable obesity-related diseases could be $66 billion a year, with the loss in economic productivity reaching between $390 billion and $580 billion annually.

That's the bad news. The good news is that this isn't one of those problems that we have to feel helpless about. As pointed out in a BAM Radio interview I conducted, we don't have a childhood obesity crisis so much as we have a physical inactivity crisis. The solution, therefore, is simple: Don't forget that the body matters, too—and get the children moving! It's what they were born to do.

What's a Teacher to Do?

• Be a role model. If kids see that the important adults in their lives value physical activity, they'll value it too. Let them know about the ways in which you're active outside of school. Display enthusiasm when they share stories about the ways in which they're physically active.

• Don't withhold recess as punishment. Conversely, never use physical activity—such as running laps or doing pushups—as punishment. It gives the impression that physical activity is something that must be suffered through.

• As best you can, contribute to the daily 60 minutes of unstructured and 60 minutes of structured physical activity recommended by SHAPE America, the association of health and physical educators.

• Don't be a bystander during recess. Circulate among the children, posing questions and challenges that encourage physical activity. Start games with them and then step out.

• Studies indicate that static playground equipment may not encourage as much physical activity as does such dynamic equipment as balls and plastic hoops. Make sure you have enough of these items to go around.

• Use transitions as an opportunity to "sneak" movement into the day. There's no reason why transitions have to involve lining up and walking. Why can't the students jog, tiptoe, or gallop to their destination? Why not move in a sideward direction? Why not pretend to walk a tightrope?

• Remember that unplanned, self-selected physical activities are not enough for young children to gain movement skills beyond an immature level. If your students don't have physical education, in addition to giving them the time, space, and opportunity to move, you should provide some basic instruction in how fundamental movement skills are performed.

• Don't forget that developmentally appropriate practice applies to movement as well. For example, the pursuit of physical fitness in childhood should not resemble the pursuit of physical fitness in adolescence or adulthood. Young children, particularly before the age of six, aren't ready for long, uninterrupted periods of strenuous activity. Also, "strength training" for children involves, not the use of equipment and weights but rather their own weight in activities they typically enjoy, such as jumping, playing tug-of-war, and pumping their legs to go higher on a swing.

• Observe children closely. You don't have to be a motor development specialist to detect potential problems. For example, if a child lands from a jump on the balls of the feet or with knees straight, help to correct those errors. If a child is having trouble with alternating movements, such as climbing or descending stairs, play games with repetitive movement patterns, such as hopscotch. If you see that a child has difficulty with certain skills, the first thing you should do is ensure more practice. If a problem seems permanent, speak with the child's parents about consulting a pediatrician, occupational therapist, or physical therapist for an evaluation.

Where to Learn More

• "Solving the Growing Physical Activity Crisis"

   www.bamradionetwork.com/educators-channel/379-solving-the-growing-physical-inactivity-crisis

• *Physical Education for Young Children: Movement ABCs for the Little Ones* by Rae Pica

• Let's Move! America's Move to Raise a Healthier Generation of Kids

   www.letsmove.gov/get-active

• SHAPE America—The Society of Health and Physical Educators

   www.shapeamerica.org

CHAPTER 15

Reading, Writing, 'Rithmetic . . . and Recess

According to the American Association for the Child's Right to Play (and, yes, it seems we do need such an organization), approximately 40 percent of U.S. elementary schools have eliminated recess from the children's day. The primary reason, of course, is the need to focus on academics and to prepare for testing. Apparently, there simply isn't time for something as "inconsequential" as recess.

It might be a reasonable argument if (a) standards and tests were all that mattered in a child's education, (b) children consisted of heads only, and (c) the research didn't confirm that children can't afford not to have recess.

Here, then, are seven contradictions to the belief that recess is inconsequential:

• Everyone benefits from a break. As far back as 1885 and 1901, the research is quite clear on this: both children and adults learn better and more quickly when their efforts are distributed (breaks are included) than when concentrated (work is conducted in longer periods). More recently, the novelty-arousal theory has suggested that people function better when they have a change of pace. Because young children don't process most information as effectively as older children (due to the immaturity of their nervous systems and their lack of experience), they can especially benefit from breaks.

• Recess increases on-task time. Dr. Olga Jarrett and her colleagues approached an urban school district with a policy against recess. They received permission for two fourth-grade classes to have recess once a week so they could determine the impact on the children's behavior on recess and non-recess days. The result was that the 43 children became more on task and less fidgety on days when they had recess. Sixty percent of the children, including the five suffering from attention deficit disorder, worked more and/or fidgeted less on recess days. Dr. Jarrett's research demonstrated that a 15-minute recess resulted in the children being five percent more on task and nine percent less fidgety, which translated into 20 minutes saved during the day.

• Children need outside light. The outside light stimulates the pineal gland, the part of the brain that helps regulate our biological clock, is vital to the immune system, and simply makes us feel better. Outside light triggers the synthesis of Vitamin D, and a number of studies have demonstrated that outside light increases academic learning and productivity as well.

• Physical activity feeds the brain. Thanks to advances in brain research, we now know that most of the brain is activated during physical activity—much more so than when doing seatwork. Also, movement increases the capacity of blood vessels (and possibly even their number), allowing for the delivery of oxygen, water, and glucose ("brain food") to the brain. This optimizes the brain's performance and may be the reason why numerous studies have shown that students who are physically active improve their academic performance, achieve higher test scores, and demonstrate a better attitude toward school. There's a reason why John Ratey, author of *Spark*, calls physical activity "Miracle-Gro for the brain."

• Unstructured play reduces stress. The National Association for the Education of Young Children (NAEYC) recommends unstructured physical play as a developmentally appropriate way of reducing stress in children's lives. Because studies show that stress has a negative impact on learning, as well as on health, we should be looking to any natural means of relieving it. For many children, especially those who are hyperactive or potentially so, recess is an opportunity to blow off steam. Outdoors, children can engage in behaviors (loud, messy, and boisterous) considered unacceptable and annoying indoors. And because recess is a break from structure and expectations, children have an opportunity to take control of their world, which is a rarity in their lives and which offers more preparation for adulthood than does memorizing the state capitals. According to one superintendent, whose letter to parents was reprinted in Lenore Skenazy's blog, *Free-Range Kids*, "Recess provides a break from instructional activities, but its lack of structure is not always most developmentally appropriate for our youngest students." Apparently he didn't read NAEYC's recommendation—and *clearly* that school administrator does not understand child development.

• Children need to learn to be social creatures. Recess may be the only time during the day when children have an opportunity to experience socialization and real communication. Neighborhoods are not what they used to be, so once the school day ends, there may be little chance for social interaction. Typically, while in school children are not allowed to interact freely during class or to talk to each other while lining up or moving from one area of the school to another. Some school policies even prevent children from talking to one another during lunch. Is it any wonder that American corporations are spending money on team-building skills for their young employees? How can children with so few opportunities to socialize and communicate be expected to live and work together as adults? When and where will they have learned how?

• Our children's health is at risk. One in six American kids is obese, according to the Robert Wood Johnson Foundation Center to Prevent Childhood Obesity. Children burn the most calories outdoors. But even children who have no weight issues require physical activity to sustain optimal health. Children who don't have the opportunity to be active during the school day don't usually compensate for that loss of activity during after-school hours. In contrast, research has shown that children who are physically active in school are more likely to be physically active at home. The outdoors is the best place for children to practice emerging physical skills and to experience the pure joy of movement, both of which increase the odds that they will become lifelong movers—and healthy adults.

Clearly, those who institute policies that eliminate recess are unfamiliar with most, if not all, of the research that I've referred to. I can't help but wonder why not when (a) some of it goes back more than a century and (b) I'd expect that those instituting policies regarding a certain subject would know a little something about the subject that they are instituting policies on.

Finally, I'd like to make three points against the practice of withholding recess as punishment—for everything from tardiness, to talking in class, to failure to complete homework:

- It doesn't teach the children anything. Withholding recess is not a logical consequence for these kinds of infractions, which renders the punishment meaningless.
- It doesn't work! Experimental studies and anecdotal evidence point out that in any given school it's generally the same children who tend to have their recess withheld, indicating that the threat is ineffective.
- Children need recess. Research, and our own common sense, tells us so (see the first list, above).

What's a Teacher to Do?

- Check out the many suggestions for advocating for recess at the website of the American Association for the Child's Right to Play (see below).

- Parents don't need research to see the effects of no-recess policies on their children because their kids come home exhausted and stressed. Still, if you provide them with information validating and reinforcing their beliefs, they'll become powerful allies for you.

- Ask administrators who have eliminated recess not only to review the research but also to recall a time when they've been forced to sit all day, whether at a meeting or on a plane. Did they wonder why they were so tired at the end of the day? It's because they were sitting all day! Research has shown that sitting makes us tired.

(Continued)

(Continued)

- If recess is offered after lunch at your school, encourage administrators to switch it to before lunch. The research shows that children who have lunch first are often shoveling their food down their throat and even throwing a lot of it away so they can go play. When they play first, they're calmer and better behaved in the cafeteria and return to the classroom more relaxed and ready to learn.

Where to Learn More

- "Why Recess Matters, How to Defend It"

  www.bamradionetwork.com/school-principals-radio/641-why-recess-matters-how-to-defend-it

- "Hey! Give Your Kids a Break!"

  www.bamradionetwork.com/educators-channel/80-hey-give-your-kids-a-break

- "The Classic Classroom Mistake and How to Avoid It"

  www.bamradionetwork.com/educators-channel/1289-the-classic-classroom-management-mistake-and-how-to-avoid-it

- "Withdrawing Recess As Punishment. Does It Work?"

  www.bamradionetwork.com/educators-channel/432-withdrawing-recess-as-punishment-does-it-work

- American Association for the Child's Right to Play

  www.ipausa.org

- "The Crucial Role of Recess in Schools"—a policy statement from the American Academy of Pediatrics (AAP)

  http://pediatrics.aappublications.org/content/131/1/183.full

CHAPTER 16

Why Kids Need "Gym"

I detested "gym" when I was in school—for a great many reasons. I didn't want to climb the rope (I was terrified of heights and rope burns), and the fact that there were 30 other kids plus the teacher scrutinizing my every move (or lack thereof) was incredibly daunting. I couldn't jump the "horse" and never understood why I had to. The sight of a dodgeball—or even a field hockey stick—headed my way instilled unspeakable fear in me. And don't get me started on waiting to be picked for a team.

So why would I be writing a piece plugging physical education (PE) for all schoolchildren? And, yes, "physical education" is the correct term for this content area, not the name of the place in which it's typically held. I guess partly for the same reason I ended up specializing in children's physical activity and teaching a required course to PE majors: life can be enormously ironic.

I certainly didn't intend to have a future involving PE. Never once, in all of my formative years, did I say to myself, "I want to be a children's physical activity specialist when I grow up." And the idea of working with university PE majors would have scared me silly—much in the way dodgeball did.

However, I've always loved to dance and that's how the whole thing began. I was 24 and taking a class in modern dance when someone asked me to teach dance to a group of local preschoolers. That sounded like a pretty cool thing to me, so I said yes. But I realized very quickly that the little ones didn't need dance technique as much as they needed basic body and spatial skills. That's when I began studying movement education—and it changed the course of my life.

So, yes, after years of learning about children and movement, I now have *plenty* of reasons why I feel strongly enough about PE—especially in the earliest grades—to advocate for it.

Let's talk about those body and spatial skills first. For young children, physical education class may be their only opportunity to acquire basic body management skills, such as body-part identification, spatial awareness, and abilities such as stopping and starting on signal. Many a child has arrived in the early- and upper-elementary grades not knowing his elbows from his shoulders, unable to line up without invading someone else's space, or lacking the ability to come to a timely halt when faced with an unexpected (or even an expected) obstacle. To many, these skills may not seem as important as those required of literacy and numeracy, but a lack of them can result in poor self-image—and *good* self-image has been linked with a child's emotional health, learning ability, and intellectual performance. Moreover, lack of these skills may well result in sedentary children who eventually become sedentary adults. People rarely partake in activities in which they feel unskilled.

And this brings us to the health reasons why children need PE. For many kids, PE class is their only opportunity to learn about the relationships between exercise, nutrition, and health. It is their only opportunity to engage in the moderate- to vigorous-intensity physical activity recommended by such organizations as the American Heart Association and others. And it may be the children's only chance to practice and refine their gross (full-body) motor skills. Even if classroom teachers are fitting fitness into the curriculum, there is still little time and space in a typical classroom for the execution of gross motor skills. And after-school physical activity programs often depend on such factors as affordability, making the cut, parent support, and transportation.

Now, you may ask, as I've come to realize many do, why you should give a fig about gross motor skills. After all, few children are going to go on to become professional athletes or dancers. Furthermore, you may believe—as many do—that children automatically acquire motor skills as their bodies develop and that it's a natural, "magical" process that occurs along with maturation.

Unfortunately, that's an easy assumption to make. After all, one day the infant rolls over, eventually begins to crawl and creep, and then, with only a little assistance and a lot of enthusiastic encouragement from adults, takes her first steps. Then, almost before we know it, she's off and running. So it indeed appears those motor skills miraculously occur and take care of themselves. To a certain extent, that's true. However, maturation takes care of only part of the process—the part that allows a child to execute most movement skills at an immature level.

What's meant by an "immature level?" It means a child who "throws like a girl" or runs "funny" or only by accident manages to connect foot to ball. It means a child who eventually loses confidence in his ability to play like the other kids. He feels clumsy and inferior and, to avoid humiliation, avoids physical activity. He simply stops moving. And having grown up with the belief that he "can't throw," "can't dance," is "uncoordinated," or "lousy at anything physical," he becomes one of the many couch potatoes among us.

Physical education class can help prevent the potato! Someone with training and know-how needs to offer children instruction, practice opportunities, assessment, and the chance to fine-tune their movement skills. Someone needs to teach young children where their elbows and shoulders are, about the space immediately surrounding their bodies (and what they're able to do within it), how to stop and start, and the many ways in which it's possible to move. Someone needs to help children retain the love of movement with which they're born so they will *keep moving*. And that someone is typically found in the school gym.

Perhaps you have the same memories of "gym class" that I have, in which case you'd be justified in wondering why, when the budget gets tight, we should continue financing the "agony" of innocent children. If so, I would suggest to you that times have changed (and so has PE). No longer do children have endless opportunities to run and jump and play; gone are the days when physical activity was a naturally occurring part of their lives. Gone are the days when the phrase "childhood obesity crisis" was unheard of. When such health risk factors as hypertension and arteriosclerosis began appearing at age 30, rather than at age five, as they do now.

Why do kids need "gym?" I would think the answer is obvious.

What's a Teacher to Do?

- Much of what you do will be determined by whether or not you have PE specialists and/or classes in your school. If you do not, please advocate for PE in whatever ways possible. Petition your administration and school board for it. If it's being put to a vote in your district, attend the meeting and make your voice heard. Solicit the support of other educators, and provide parents with information and research backing PE.

- If your students don't participate in PE, find ways to fit fitness into the classroom. Take brain breaks involving moderate- to vigorous-intensity physical activity (running in place, jumping or skipping around the perimeter of the room, dancing to lively music, and the like). Take advantage of transitions to promote body and spatial awareness; for example, invite the students to move in backward or sideward directions, at a low or high level in space, on only three body parts, and so forth.

- When your students are outdoors, circulate among them, issuing challenges and asking questions that prompt more movement. Start and/or play active games with them such as Follow the Leader, being sure to include gross motor skills and changes in direction and level among your movements. Modify games that involve elimination so every child has an opportunity for continuous participation. For instance, children who most need to practice their listening and body-part identification skills are typically the first to be eliminated from Simon Says. But if you instead arrange the children in two circles or lines, those who respond without Simon's "permission" can simply move from their circle or line to the other and continue playing the game.

Where to Learn More

- "Why Play Time Is Not Break Time"

  www.bamradionetwork.com/educators-channel/642-why-play-time-is-not-break-time

- "Building Your Child's Physical Foundation"

  www.bamradionetwork.com/movement-play/340-building-your-childs-physical-foundation

- "The Importance of Physical Education"

  www.veanea.org/home/1000.htm

PART III

Understanding Developmentally Appropriate Practice

CHAPTER 17

In Defense of Authentic Learning

As I started to write this piece, it struck me that the title I'd chosen is an interesting one. I mean, why would authentic learning have to be defended? If authentic means "real or genuine," as it's defined in the dictionary, how could anybody object? Who wouldn't want children to have real, genuine learning?

Well, apparently some don't. Clearly there are a whole lot of policymakers and education reformers out there who are only interested in how well students swallow and regurgitate data. If that were not the case, they wouldn't require students to take such an obscene number of tests. They wouldn't tie performance on those tests to teacher evaluations. They wouldn't force teachers to implement scripted curriculums. They wouldn't find it reasonable to require all students to know all of the same things all at the same time.

And parents, who don't understand that memorization isn't necessarily synonymous with real learning, are also too often enamored of the recitation of facts. If their children can say their ABCs, recite the state capitals, and count to 100—in two languages—they're satisfied that knowledge has been imparted. But feats such as this represent only *rote* learning. Most parents don't realize that until there's comprehension, there's no authentic learning taking place.

Until a child grasps what the numbers, letters, or words represent—until the information has some relevance to the child's life—there'll be no true learning. This, of course, is why a mother not long ago called me out when I tweeted about project-based learning, insisting that it was "nonsense."

I'm not saying that rote learning doesn't have its place. It's how most of us learned the multiplication tables and significant dates in history. However, unless a child is going to grow up to become a contestant on television game shows, memorizing facts will have little use in life once she or he has passed all of the tests that schools require.

The truth is, in today's digital age, there's far less need for memorization of facts than in the days when one had to own an expensive set of encyclopedias or travel to a library to find answers. Today, if facts are needed, one has only to type a keyword or two into a search box on whatever piece of digital equipment is handy and the answer will "magically" appear. Yes, there will always be careers requiring the memorization of information (chemists must know the table of elements, language teachers certain grammatical rules, and doctors symptoms), but I don't think it's an exaggeration to say that every current and future career—every life path students will choose to follow—will require less data recollection and more of the ability to solve problems.

And where are today's students learning to solve problems? Not in school, where following directions and filling in bubbles are taking up the majority of their time. As Will Richardson said in a TEDx Talk, "Test prep and learning are two very different things and one is being lost at the expense of the other right now."

As has been the case for more than a century, most of today's schools are cramming students' heads with all of the same information, as though kids are indistinguishable from one another, and as though they are all going to make the exact same choices once they graduate. Those choices may have been far more limited when our system of education was devised—when many students would leave school to work in mass production assembly lines—but that is not today's world. It's a fact that given the current rate of change, today's world will not be tomorrow's. In actuality, given the current rate of change, we have no idea what the world will look like when today's students graduate. When we consider the prediction that 65 percent of current elementary school students will end up doing jobs that have yet to be invented, we have to ask, as did Will Richardson, if we really want our kids being prepped for their future by a system that hasn't fundamentally changed in 125 years.

How many things can you name that *have* changed in 125 years? The mind boggles to consider it. Yet our system of education hasn't? That's nearly impossible to wrap one's thoughts around.

Only by showing students *how* to learn as we simultaneously encourage them what to learn, by giving them real-world problems to solve, by allowing them to investigate interesting questions, by encouraging them to follow their passions and interests, and by fostering the love of learning they were born with, can we best prepare them for an unknowable future.

When we guide students through the process of exploration and discovery and the resulting knowledge has real-world implications, that is authentic learning and *that* will serve a child for a lifetime.

What's a Teacher to Do?

- Implement true project-based learning, which allows students to create "meaningful content," as teacher Josh Stumpenhorst recommended in a BAM interview. Josh went on to talk about students "creating something that's going to do something for the world, for their community, and for themselves." The learning can't get any more authentic than that—and you *can* design projects with these standards in mind.

- Permit students to investigate problems over an extended period of time. Real problems can't be solved in a class period or two.

- Use technology to enable your students to engage with mentors and other students from around the world.

- Make movements such as Genius Hour (see below) part of your classroom.

Where to Learn More

- "Helping Parents Understand the New Strategies for Teaching and Learning"

  www.bamradionetwork.com/index.php?option=com_content&view=article&id=2158:working-toward-a-common-goal-more-important-than-working-toward-an-qaq&catid=35:jackstreet54&Itemid=89

- "Bringing Authenticity to the Classroom"

  www.edutopia.org/blog/bringing-authenticity-to-the-classroom-andrew-miller

- Genius Hour

  www.geniushour.com/

- "Encouraging Children's Ability to Think"—with Lilian Katz

  www.bamradionetwork.com/educators-channel/160-encouraging-childrens-ability-to-think

- Will Richardson's TEDx Talk

  www.youtube.com/watch?v=Ni75vIE4vdk

- "Worksheets: Bad? Good? Well, It Depends . . . "

  www.bamradionetwork.com/educators-channel/266-worksheets-bad-good-depends

CHAPTER 18

Who Should Lead the Learning?

"We all talk about wanting independent thinkers, but we don't actually allow them to do that in school."

Those are the words of teacher Josh Stumpenhorst in a BAM Radio segment called, "Trusting Students to Lead Their Learning." They follow very much in the same vein as those of Donald Trefinger, author of *Creative Problem Solving*, who has written,

> Pupils learn from the primary grades that someone else, usually the teacher, who is presumed to be the wisest person in the room, knows best what they should do, how and when it should be done, and when it has been completed satisfactorily. Instead of learning to be critical, imaginative, and independent, there is too often an emphasis on being obedient, cooperative, and dependent.

We, as a society, know that today's world benefits far more from creative, independent thinkers than it does from those who are only capable of blindly following orders and looking to someone else for answers. Still, our system of education prepares students considerably more for the latter scenario than for the former. Preservice training has long taught future educators to stand in front of the class and disseminate information—to be the "sage on the stage" and to convey the impression that only through them can students come to know anything of value.

Given this long-standing approach, it's no wonder that many teachers feel less than confident about handing the reins to their students—about being the "guide on the side." Will they still be needed in a classroom where students are leading their own learning?

The answer to that question is *yes*. Stumpenhorst, who throughout the entire third trimester of his language arts class does not organize any whole-class lessons but, rather, invites the kids to take the standards and create their own learning syllabus, says he is still needed in a different capacity. He's no longer providing the answers, but he is providing questions and helping students discover the tools to answer them.

And it's paying off. Josh insists that by sitting next to students rather than standing in front of them, the kids have "learned a whole lot more." He has the numbers to support that as well as the anecdotal information. And his contention concurs with the research, which has demonstrated that students learn better when they learn on their own or from each other.

Instructional coach David Ginsburg, in that same BAM interview, said that some people think students are incapable of learning on their own or from each other, but the real issue isn't whether students are able to learn independently; it's whether teachers are ready and willing to let them. Panelist Alan November, author of *Who Owns the Learning?*, insisted that students don't need teachers to be their source of information; they need teachers to facilitate the process of getting that information. When I asked him why it was important for students to be able to lead their own learning, he simply stated, "Because one day they're not going to have their teacher."

Works for me.

Noted early childhood educator Lilian Katz, in a much earlier BAM interview, spoke with me about the difference between intellectual goals and academic ones. The latter, she says, involve acquiring bits of information unrelated to one another. The former involve the functions of the mind in their fullest sense. Academic skills, Katz said, should be used in *service* of the intellect. She implored listeners not to underestimate children and their capacity to get absorbed and to try to analyze things on their own.

If intellectual, versus academic, goals are what we're aiming for in education, I would say that the answer to the question posed in the title of this piece is fairly evident.

What's a Teacher to Do?

• Know your students and meet them where they are, whether that means they need you to be completely hands-on, to get completely out of the way, or to be somewhere in the middle. For those in the first group, you should strive to build their ability to one day work independently (from Josh Stumpenhorst).

• Know your objectives going in, but then let go a little and see what the kids are interested in (from teacher Ariel Sacks).

• Don't do anything for the students that they can do for themselves, and don't answer questions that they're able to answer on their own. Josh says that throughout the entire year he's "un-brainwashing" them from their reliance on the teacher for all of the answers.

• According to David Ginsburg, student-centered learning doesn't have to be a complete pedagogical shift. He recommends, among other things, giving kids "think-alone" time and not ending a discussion after one student has answered a question.

• Ask more questions where there are no right answers or where there are multiple strategies for getting at the right answer. Be open to kids' responses and validate those responses (from David Ginsburg).

• "Ask, don't tell." Instead of disseminating information, figure out a question that lets the students arrive at it on their own (from David Ginsburg).

• Give a homework assignment every day requiring each student to ask a question. If you gather a question every day from every student, you'll better know how to help guide them (from Alan November).

Where to Learn More

- "Trusting Students to Lead Their Learning: Does It Really Work? If So, How?"

  www.bamradionetwork.com/educators-channel/1276-trusting-students-to-lead-their-learning-does-it-really-work-if-so-how

- "Is the Sage on the Stage Really Dead? Well, Almost . . . "

  www.bamradionetwork.com/educators-channel/1145-is-the-sage-on-the-stage-really-dead-yes-well-almost

- "Encouraging Children's Ability to Think"—with Lilian Katz

  www.bamradionetwork.com/educators-channel/160-encouraging-childrens-ability-to-think

- *The Passion-Driven Classroom: A Framework for Teaching and Learning* by Angela Maiers and Amy Sandvold

CHAPTER 19

The Trouble With Testing

For the second time, I find myself questioning title selection. The trouble with testing? Where to begin? How does one convey, in approximately a thousand words, all the "trouble" associated with testing, when an entire series of very large books could easily be devoted to the subject—one to each "trouble?"

In truth, there already has been a great deal written about the problems associated with too much testing. Still, the use of standardized tests in the United States proliferates rather than diminishes. Americans, it seems, have an ever-increasing obsession with measuring and quantifying things. As evidence of this, consider that nowhere else in the world do standardized tests play such a large role in education. According to a study from the Brookings Institute in 2012, we were at the time spending $1.7 billion annually on standardized tests in public schools. And a new study, from the Center for American Progress, has found that U.S. students are tested an average of once a month, with some tested as often as twice a month.

Of course, none of this indicates how much time U.S. students spend *readying* for tests, in addition to taking them. According to the Center for American Progress study, some states and districts highlight testing above learning, devoting time to test prep, practice tests, and even pep rallies. As someone who thoroughly enjoyed pep rallies for football games in high school, I'm conjuring up a very weird image of marching bands and cheerleaders trying to generate excitement for filling in bubbles.

And all of this is despite what numerous experts have had to say: standardized tests are indicative of neither intelligence nor potential.

According to Peter Sacks, author of *Standardized Minds: The High Price of America's Testing Culture and What We Can Do to Change It*, although the claim is that standardized tests determine a person's potential for later success in school, college, and life, their actual ability to do so has been "awful." As one example, Sacks points to the fact that women perform consistently worse on college entrance exams than men, yet women consistently surpass men in their actual performance in college. Sacks says the "poor ability of the exams to tell us much about later performance has been true both for people who score well on standardized tests and those who do not."

And what about the ability of standardized tests to measure intelligence?

Those who understand intelligence know that it doesn't involve the mere accumulation of information. Intelligence involves knowing how to acquire information you don't yet possess and, most important, knowing how to *use* it once you've got it. In fact, there is a statistical link between high scores on standardized tests and what is considered "shallow" thinking. Too often, those who score well are simply good at memorizing or at guessing which multiple-choice answers should be marked. Standardized tests do *not* require the understanding, creative thinking, analysis, synthesis, or application of information that are the hallmarks of in-depth thinking (you know, the kind we need to continue to innovate and prosper).

Moreover, standardized tests promote the myth of "one right answer." Yes, two plus two will always equal four, and the right combination of hydrogen and oxygen will always produce water. But there is a real danger to our children if they grow up believing there is one right answer to *every* question or problem.

First and foremost, when children become convinced of the value of one right answer, what becomes of their critical thinking skills? How can they trust in their ability to solve problems? Business leaders, in fact, are already finding themselves among such people. One of their chief complaints about today's young employees is their inability to think creatively and to communicate. Interesting, considering the many business leaders behind the push for greater accountability.

And what of the content of these tests? How valuable is it in preparing our kids for their future?

To answer that question, I share two of the (among many) ridiculous and disturbing stories I've heard about the content of standardized tests. The first took place in Midland, Texas, where four-year-olds in a Head Start program were required to take the new formal tests that are now, thankfully, no longer required. The tests were verbal rather than written, but that seemed to be the only concession made to the children's stage of development. Not only were these little ones expected to be able to interpret graphs (a skill requiring highly developed logical/mathematical, and visual/spatial intelligences), but they were also supposed to be able to describe a swamp.

Perhaps it's just me, but I think that would be a challenge for anyone of any age. What *are* the right words to describe a swamp? Moreover, the test makers had failed to consider that such a question would be especially challenging for these children—because they lived in *Midland, Texas*, a place known far more for tumbleweeds than for anything wet. A place so dry that unless its young residents had experienced travel that included swampland, there was no reason for them to ever have heard the word *swamp*.

The second story came to me via a mom. Her son had taken a standardized test in which one of the questions was the following: What are windows made of? Her son checked "glass" as the answer—which seems entirely logical to me. Unfortunately, the test makers considered windows to be made up of "squares," so his answer was scored as incorrect.

As the lawyers say, I rest my case.

Noted educator David Elkind declared in a BAM Radio interview, "Learning how to take tests is not what gets you ahead in the world, particularly in a global economy."

Despite the truth so clearly evident in that statement—and despite the fact that decades of testing have done nothing to improve our children's education—the politicians and policymakers still pound podiums in their righteous insistence that "more testing" is what we need for advancement in our classrooms.

What is it that they say about the definition of insanity? Oh, yes: it's doing the same thing over and over again and expecting different results.

What's a Teacher to Do?

• Rebel. Teachers in Seattle high schools determined that the MAP tests were inconsequential and costly, both in terms of money and time; so they banded together and boycotted them. If there are tests about which you feel similarly, find likeminded colleagues (don't do it alone) who will join you in refusing to administer them.

• Show administrators and policymakers the results of more "formative" assessments: the curriculum-based projects and tests you give to your students throughout the year. Help them to see the value of this kind of feedback on how students are progressing.

• Many parents are protesting overtesting and keeping their kids home from school on test days. Other parents instruct their children to answer only half of the questions on a standardized test. Let parents know of these options.

• Invite policymakers into your classroom on test-prep or testing days so they can see for themselves what it looks like. Tell them your stories and those of your students. Then invite them to return on days when authentic learning is taking place so they have a basis for comparison.

• To the extent possible, make test prep engaging and fun. In a BAM segment, three teachers insisted it doesn't have to be only drill-and-kill and offered suggestions for taking test prep beyond that.

Where to Learn More

- "Ten Ways to Make Test Prep Fun"

  www.bamradionetwork.com/teachers-aid/1871-ten-ways-to-make-test-prep-fun

- "A Ridiculous Common Core Test for First Graders"

  www.washingtonpost.com/blogs/answer-sheet/wp/2013/10/31/a-ridiculous-common-core-test-for-first-graders/

- "A New York and Chicago Mom Discover What Standardized Rigor Really Means for Their Children"

  http://missourieducationwatchdog.com/a-new-york-and-chicago-mom-discover-what-standardized-rigor-really-means-for-their-children/

- "Testing 1, 2, 3: Accountability Run Amok"

  www.ecepolicymatters.com/archives/757

- "Unions Say They Will Back Teachers Who Refuse to Administer Mandated Standardized Tests to Students"

  www.washingtonpost.com/blogs/answer-sheet/wp/2014/10/06/unions-say-they-will-back-teachers-who-refuse-to-administer-mandated-standardized-tests-to-students/

- "How to End Over-Testing in Schools: Kids Should Answer Only Half the Questions"

  www.commondreams.org/views/2013/04/30/how-end-over-testing-schools-kids-should-answer-only-half-questions

CHAPTER 20

Failure
Is an Option

"Yesterday the kids came in for their first-grade music class all hot and sweaty from 'running' the quarter-mile 'race' around the bus loop. One little peanut, not bigger than a minute, said to me, 'Yeah, I failed.'"

Sadly, stories (feelings) such as this are not unusual. I've witnessed children as young as four and five years old afraid of being wrong or looking foolish. They're the children who sit on the sidelines rather than participate in something new and unfamiliar—even though they may be aching to join the fun. They're the ones who never speak up. They're the ones who color strictly within the lines.

Where do children of such a tender age learn that failing to come in first is *failing*, and that making a mistake is the worst thing they can do?

Everywhere, it seems. Their home and school experiences have taught them that "effortless perfection" is the goal and that anything short of that is to be avoided at all costs. Indeed, many of today's parents not only go to endless effort to protect their children from potential harm (real or imagined), they also go to extremes to ensure their children are protected from making mistakes—either out of fear that their children will fall apart should they prove to be imperfect or out of the belief that perfection is the only route to a successful future. Consider the story I once heard about former president Ronald Reagan asking an Olympic silver medalist how it felt to "lose," and you'll grasp our culture's attitude toward anything other than being number one.

And, of course, in school there are serious consequences for making mistakes. Make one in front of the whole class and you're likely to feel humiliated. Make one on a test or assignment and you get a bad grade. Make too many of them, and not only are you susceptible to the teacher's disapproval, these days you may even cost your teacher her job!

Alina Tugend, author of *Better by Mistake: The Unexpected Benefits of Being Wrong*, said in a BAM interview that as a result of all the pressure placed on them to be perfect, today's children lack resiliency, a key characteristic in happy, successful adults. The first time they make a big mistake, they fall apart. Additionally, she said, we're raising a generation of kids afraid to take risks and to try creative things. They just want to "stick to what they know, pass that test, get that A, and move on."

That attitude probably will not get them very far in life. But that attitude is far too often what's being fostered in homes and schools in this country.

An elementary school music teacher told me the story with which I opened this piece. She wisely advised the little girl that she absolutely had not failed—that trying was what mattered. Motivation expert Carol Dweck would have approved. Dweck is the psychology professor behind the notion of a *growth*, as opposed to a *fixed*, mindset.

With the latter, individuals believe that such basic attributes as intelligence and talent are predetermined and invariable. Therefore, they don't see the value of effort and tend to spend all of their time proving their intelligence or talent instead of trying to develop them.

Conversely, those with a growth mindset believe in the value of hard work. They understand that intelligence and talent can be bettered with effort. According to Dweck, this mindset has been fundamental to the success of all great people.

While conducting research for her theory, Dweck asked 400 New York City fifth graders to take a short, easy test in which almost all of them performed well. Half the children were praised for being really smart; the other half were complimented for working really hard. The students were then asked to take a second test. They could choose easy or hard. Almost all of those praised for being smart chose the easy test because they didn't want to look dumb. Almost all of those praised for working really hard chose the more challenging test.

In a BAM interview, Dweck told me, "Praising their intelligence or talent made them vulnerable. They didn't want to take on a challenge and they felt bad about themselves when they made a mistake. Children who were praised for their *effort* or their strategy—something about the process they were engaged in—remained very challenge-seeking. They loved learning, and they were resilient when they had setbacks."

That's a good enough argument for me.

In the process of writing her book, Alina Tugend discovered that other cultures have a different view of mistakes. Where we in North America see them as failures, in such places as China and Japan they're an indicator of what still needs to be learned.

What a lovely—and sensible—way of looking at things.

What's a Teacher to Do?

- Encourage and support rather than praise.

- Make sure your actions match your words. If you say that it's okay to make mistakes but react in a way that contradicts that, the children will pick up on the latter.

- Let children know that you *expect* them to make mistakes—that we especially make mistakes when we're taking a risk or trying something new. Einstein once said that anybody who never made a mistake had never tried anything new.

- Remember that the process (the learning!) is far more important than the product (the end result, or grade). To the extent possible, help parents understand this as well.

- Don't try to hide it when *you* make a mistake. Send the clear message that adults make them, too, and that it's no big deal.

Where to Learn More

- "Victims of Excellence: Teaching Children to Learn from Mistakes, Parents to Allow Them"

  www.bamradionetwork.com/educators-channel/731-victims-of-excellence-teaching-children-to-learn-from-mistakes-parents-to-allow-them

- "The Dangers of Praising Children Inappropriately" with Carol Dweck

  www.bamradionetwork.com/educators-channel/162-the-dangers-of-praising-children-inappropriately

- "Good Teachers, Great Teachers, Perfect Teachers: Which One Doesn't Exist?"

  www.bamradionetwork.com/educators-channel/2297-good-teachers-great-teachers-perfect-teachers-which-one-doesnt-exist

- "7 Crippling Parenting Behaviors That Keep Children from Growing into Leaders"

  www.forbes.com/sites/kathycaprino/2014/01/16/7-crippling-parenting-behaviors-that-keep-children-from-growing-into-leaders/

- "It's a Mistake Not to Use Mistakes As Part of the Learning Process"

  www.edutopia.org/blog/use-mistakes-in-learning-process-richard-curwin

CHAPTER 21

Should We Teach Handwriting in the Digital Age?

I n June of 2011, the Indiana Department of Education joined the ranks of school systems that no longer required the teaching of cursive writing. In a memo sent to school leaders, the department stated that in accordance with the Common Core standards, students will be "expected to become proficient in keyboarding skills," rather than handwriting.

In February of 2013, the Indiana Senate voted to advance a "cursive bill" requiring schools to teach cursive writing, reversing the 2011 decision.

This, in a nutshell, sums up the handwriting debate erupting across the country in the 21st century.

Should schools continue to teach handwriting in the digital age? When I asked the question in a segment for BAM Radio, I was surprised that none of the three panelists felt as strongly as I did about maintaining the tradition.

Steve Graham, professor of special education and literacy at Vanderbilt University, whose research interests include writing instruction and development, said that we're using a 20th-century tool in a 21st-century world and that we really need to step up to the current century. Lisa Guernsey, director of the Early Education Initiative at the New America Foundation, pointed out that children want to keyboard, to write more fluently and get ideas out of their heads as fast as possible. And Anne Trubek, an associate professor of rhetoric and composition at Oberlin College, was outspoken in her view that we do away with handwriting instruction. She stated the following:

> We have these larger cultural connections to handwriting as a sense of identity and self-expression. It has to be put into the context of nostalgia and history and separated from educational goals.

After the segment went live on the BAM website, I started an online forum discussion on the topic and was stunned, not only by the number of comments but also by the passion with which educators approached the topic—on both sides. I was gratified to find *some* support here.

On the "con" side, it was argued that handwriting will soon be as obsolete as hunting for food with a bow and arrow and that those concerned with a small child's inability to reach all of the keys on a keyboard should think about "moving forward"—by making "baby keyboards." Do we really want children spending even *more* time in front of screens?

One respondent countered:

> Make all the esoteric arguments you like. This is something that affects students NOW. I tutor many children who still have to get by in a pencil and paper world—and many of them are functionally crippled by the act of handwriting. They must hand write responses in their testing booklets and without proper handwriting skills, they write incomplete thoughts—sketchy frameworks and wisps of ideas—rather than fight the muscle fatigue. Unless it's possible (or even desirable) for students to use only keyboards or touch screens at all times, proper handwriting must remain a valued skill.

As for me, I firmly believe that we must keep handwriting instruction in the curriculum.

It's true that I've been accused on several occasions of being old-fashioned, particularly when it comes to the use of technology (especially in early education). But having spent 35 years specializing in the education of the whole child, I know it's necessary for children to have as many fine- and gross-motor experiences as possible! And I'm not going to apologize for it.

Indeed, Christy Isbell, a pediatric occupational therapist, confirmed for me that handwriting promotes manipulation and finger isolation skills that are useful for other fine-motor activities, including self-care *and* use of technology. And I know from my own work that learning to write by hand has a positive impact on emergent literacy, as it gives children an important opportunity to physically experience the spatial orientation and directionality of letters in a way that keyboarding simply can't.

A policy update on the handwriting debate from the National Association of State Boards of Education (NASBE) in September of 2012 pointed out several educational benefits of learning to write by hand. They included cognitive development, motor skills development, literacy development, written expression, memory, and brain development.

Regarding the latter, Virginia Berninger, a professor of psychology at the University of Washington, has written that cursive writing in particular is linked to self-regulation and mental organization.

And neurophysiologist Carla Hannaford told me in an e-mail that the research

> around the area of the brain dedicated to the hand (both sensory and motor) shows that the hand is essential to both verbalization and increased creative thought . . . Also, we know that cursive writing activates both hemispheres of the brain—and that carpal bone development in the hand is very slow. Printing and typing take much more carpal bone development than does cursive writing.

It is research such as this that's prompting states to reconsider—and reverse—decisions to remove handwriting instruction from the curriculum.

With all due respect to Anne Trubek, this is about more than nostalgia.

I'll admit that recently, as I crafted a handwritten thank you note to a conference organizer who'd invited me to deliver a keynote, I pondered how sad it would be if in the future, no one ever received a note written by hand. So, yes, nostalgia plays a part in my thinking. But, beyond that, I worry that we can be too quick to embrace the latest technologies without considering the long-term consequences (it is so easy to succumb to the lure of the newest gadgets), and it is my hope that schools will not look at cursive and keyboarding as an either/or proposition.

Yes, keyboarding is quicker—and we are a nation in a hurry. But faster isn't always better. And are there not some things that nature intended that technology can't replace? I mean, if we all had access to Segways, would we simply stop walking?

What's a Teacher to Do?

- If handwriting instruction is frowned upon by your school or district, use the information below (I recently conducted a second radio program in order to serve the cause) to advocate for it. Take the research to your administrators and school board. Write letters to the newspaper or blog about it online. Garner support via social media, which is a powerful way to create change in this day and age.

- Present the research to parents. They want the best for their children and may be your greatest allies.

- Teach it anyway. And if that's truly not possible, provide parents with information on how they can offer the instruction at home.

Where to Learn More

- "Why Handwriting Still Matters in the Digital Age"

  www.bamradionetwork.com/educators-channel/2167-why-handwriting-still-matters-in-the-digital-age

- "The Handwriting Debate"—a policy update from the NASBE

  www.hw21summit.com/media/zb/hw21/H2989_NASBE_PolicyUpdate_TheHandwritingDebate.pdf

- "Can You Imagine the World Without Handwriting?"

  www.hw21summit.com/

- "Why Learning to Write by Hand Matters"

  www.edweek.org/ew/articles/2014/03/12/24vachon.h33.html

- "What's Lost As Handwriting Fades"

  www.nytimes.com/2014/06/03/science/whats-lost-as-handwriting-fades.html?_r=0

CHAPTER 22

Just Say "No" to Keyboarding in Kindergarten

Throughout the country over the past few years, state departments of education and school leaders have been determining that in accordance with the Common Core Standards, students should be required to become proficient with keyboarding skills rather than handwriting. That, of course, raises the question: If handwriting is no longer to be used as a form of communication but the computer is, at what age should children be learning keyboarding skills?

It's an especially important question considering a colleague's story about her first-grade grandson being given an assignment meant to be word-processed on the computer. Strangely, his class had received no keyboarding instruction prior to this—which meant that success was highly unlikely. But my colleague's primary concern was that "hunt-and-peck" would become her grandson's "default brain template." This, she feared, would make it more difficult for him and his classmates to acquire the proper keyboarding techniques that would later save time and prevent repetitive injuries.

Naturally, I decided a radio segment on the topic was in order. My guests for "Is Teaching Keyboarding in Kindergarten Developmentally Appropriate?" were Jacqui Murray, a K–5 tech teacher; Cris Rowan, a pediatric occupational therapist; and Lisa Guernsey, a regular on-air commentator for BAM Radio Network, an expert in early childhood matters and the mother of two young girls.

When I addressed my colleague's concern, Jacqui confirmed that it is absolutely essential that children learn to type in the right way—that if they aren't taught to use all of their fingers, they frequently can't escape the hunt-and-peck pattern. Indeed, she's witnessed many fifth-graders with exactly that problem.

So, what age should children be learning keyboarding skills? If first-grade teachers are going to assign work meant to be word-processed, it would seem that the answer is *in kindergarten*.

Wrong.

Although the experts aren't actually in agreement when it comes to the start of formal keyboarding lessons, no one with any credibility is recommending typing instruction for the little, uncoordinated hands of a kindergartner. Many say formal lessons should not start until fourth or fifth grade, with the earliest recommendation I've come across being third grade. As Jacqui pointed out, "Finger placement and touch typing in kindergarten would be absurd."

What many people fail to realize is that there are natural laws at play here. Developmental patterns cannot—and should not—be rushed. Control over the body occurs from top (head) to bottom (toes), from the middle (trunk) to the outside (extremities), and from large body parts (trunk, neck, arms, legs) to small body parts (fingers, hands, toes, wrists, eyes). Once we understand this progression, we can grasp why Cris Rowan insists that young children learn their keyboarding skills *on the playground*. It may seem like a bizarre contention, but she's absolutely correct when she states that children must first develop their core muscles and gross motor (large-muscle) skills before we can expect them to master tasks requiring fine motor skills.

In fact, Cris tells us that because today's children are spending so much time in front of screens and *not* on the playground, they don't have the muscle tone "integral for the development of motor coordination." She cited a 2009 study stating that due to technology overuse, one-third of children entering school are developmentally delayed. The last thing they need is to spend more time in front of screens.

Despite some belief to the contrary, I do know and accept that technology is going to be part of children's lives. And I realize, as Lisa Guernsey pointed out, that children become excited about using computers. But they become excited about Halloween candy, too; that doesn't mean we adults are going to indulge their desire to eat it all in one sitting. And just because the *things* in children's lives have changed, it doesn't mean the children themselves have. The laws of nature and child development still apply.

Bottom line, keyboarding should *not* be taught in kindergarten—and first-grade teachers should not be giving assignments meant to be completed on a keyboard.

Honestly, if I had my way, there wouldn't even *be* computers in kindergarten classrooms. Believe it or not, children learn just fine without them. They'd likely not even miss them. And they'd certainly have more time and desire to be on the playground.

That conviction doesn't make me popular among some of my colleagues—but that's my story and I'm sticking to it.

What's a Teacher to Do?

• Remember—and promote the idea—that as Cris Rowan told listeners, when a child is developmentally ready to do something, he or she will do it.

• Be aware of the balance between screen time and "big body play" among your students.

• Learn what you can about the importance and progression of fine motor skills. Make the development of fine motor skills part of your curriculum. You can integrate this with academics but should always make practice playful as opposed to rote and boring.

• Advocate for a "progressive approach" that's age and developmentally appropriate to learning keyboarding skills at your school. It's not enough to be doing the right thing in your classroom; there has to be continuity from one grade to the next.

Where to Learn More

- "Is Teaching Keyboarding in Kindergarten Developmentally Appropriate?"

  www.bamradionetwork.com/educators-channel/738-is-teaching-keyboarding-in-kindergarten-developmentally-appropriate

- *Virtual Child: The Terrifying Truth About What Technology Is Doing to Children* by Cris Rowan

- "Fine Motor Skills: What Are They, Why Are They Too Important to Overlook?"

  www.bamradionetwork.com/educators-channel/774-fine-motor-skills-what-are-they-why-are-they-too-important-to-overlook

- *Mighty Fine Motor Skills: Fine Motor Activities for Young Children* by pediatric occupational therapist (OT) Christy Isbell

CHAPTER 23

iPads or Play-Doh?

The topic of technology in classrooms, particularly early childhood classrooms, has created quite a ruckus among educators—with no end in sight.

At one end of the spectrum are those who firmly believe that if technology is going to be part of children's lives (and it is), they must begin experiencing and exploring it in their earliest years. At the other end of the spectrum are those who firmly believe that children will have the rest of their lives to stick their heads in the "sand" that is technology. They believe that early childhood is typically the only phase in one's life during which it's possible to experience life fully and joyously, via all of the senses and that precious time shouldn't be spent in a two-dimensional world.

Of course, there will always be those who call for balance. Typically, I'm among them. The National Association for the Education of Young Children (NAEYC), the country's largest organization of early childhood professionals, advocates for "both/and" thinking, as opposed to "either/or." They recommend that early childhood educators use technology in meaningful, developmentally appropriate ways. Their executive director, Rhian Evans Allvin, wrote of children "in an American city visiting with their peers in a remote Eastern European community through Skype," or a teacher "integrating a smart board with touchscreen technology in a group lesson about democratic society." She cited these examples as representing "the integration of technology in ways designed not to replace human interaction but to enhance it."

Sounds wonderful. But the cynic in me wants to jump up and down and remind everyone that few people are familiar enough with developmentally appropriate practice in general, let alone where technology is concerned. The cynic in me wants to jump up and down and remind everyone she's actually seen very little in the way of balance in this country. *Extremes*, that's what we're about. We're all-in or all-out. And when we get excited about something—as we do about the many new gadgets available to us—it's definitely all-in.

Today's young parents, unfortunately, typically lean toward the all-in end of the spectrum, displaying great enthusiasm for shiny new gizmos, as well as for "learning tools" for their children. They're spending billions of dollars on electronic "educational products," both in order to give their children a head start in life and to keep the little ones occupied while they do other things. I'm also seeing far too many parents fail to engage with their children because they're too busy engaging with their fancy phones. The young father I see when I walk in the morning is just one sad example. He's pushing a baby carriage and holding the dog's leash with one hand while clasping his telephone up to his face with the other hand. Not only is he blissfully unaware of his beautiful surroundings, there also is no interaction—no language spoken—with that baby. I want to shake him out of his stupor and ask what could be so important on that device that he can't take his face away from it for the few minutes it takes to go for a walk.

Cris Rowan, pediatric occupational therapist, author of *Virtual Child* and a guest on BAM Radio, worries that as parents become addicted to their devices (and they do) so, too, do children, in the absence of a parent's attention. She told listeners, "Children are disconnecting from parents, from each other, from teachers, and it's causing a whole host of problems in health and education."

Wouldn't it be lovely if the early childhood classroom could be a place where kids got a reprieve from the excess of electronic stimulation they're getting at home—and, now, even in the car? Don't get me started on that topic.

Jane Healy, author of *Failure to Connect: How Computers Affect Our Children's Minds—and What We Can Do About It*, insists there's no need for children to be exposed to computers before the age of seven. And I agree. It makes perfect sense when we stop to consider what we know about child and brain development and how children learn: through all of their senses, through movement, and through social interaction. All of that is limited when children spend their time with screens. And for those who insist that children need to become accustomed to tech in their earliest years, I have two arguments: Bill Gates and Steve Jobs. Neither of them had access to tech when they were children (because it didn't exist), and as we all know they did quite well with it in their later years.

Besides, with the rapid and crazy rate at which technology is changing, almost every electronic thing children experience today will be obsolete tomorrow.

What are some of the other arguments in favor of low- or no-tech in early childhood? They include

- ocular lock and other vision problems created when one sits motionless staring at a flat screen;
- the lack of physical activity contributing to an already overwhelming obesity problem;
- the recent report that fine motor control is negatively impacted by the amount of time infants and toddlers are spending with tablets and touchscreens;
- the lack of research determining the long-term consequences of exposure to electronic devices;
- the fact that Steve Jobs himself limited technology usage for his children at home and many other tech giants do the same; and
- even Silicon Valley tech executives send their kids to tech-free schools!

I realize that among my tech-loving colleagues I'm considered a "dinosaur," a "technophobe," and probably some other labels I haven't been privy to. But I take comfort in the fact that there are many people I admire—people far more knowledgeable than I—who stand with me on the same side of this issue.

I *do* believe in balance. But balance, at least in the United States, is as rare as Sasquatch sightings, and in the absence of it I'm duty-bound to lean toward the no-tech end of the spectrum. The questions I encourage every parent and early childhood professional to ponder are the following: Is there danger to children from too little use of technology? Is there danger to children from too much technology use? If you answered *no* and *absolutely*, as I do, then there's really no debate here: it's Play-Doh over iPads every time.

> ## What's a Teacher to Do?
>
> • Our brand new world requires brand new learning. If you plan to introduce technology into your classroom—at whatever grade level—seek training in how best to do so. And, because tech is changing so rapidly, stay up to date on tools and the best practices for using them.
>
> • Make it a policy to enhance, not replace. Technology is a tool and, as such, should be used to enrich the teaching and learning experience, not substitute for it.
>
> • Start small. If you decide to bring technology into your classroom—at any grade level—determine what you want to teach and what one tool can help you do it more effectively.
>
> • If you're in an early childhood classroom and decide to go technology free, stand tall and know that you're not alone in your decision to allow young children to experience life in three dimensions. Seek the support of other likeminded individuals. Collect enough data to reinforce your position should it be questioned by parents or administrators.

Where to Learn More

- "5 Ways Technology May Adversely Alter Child Development"

  www.bamradionetwork.com/educators-channel/588-5-ways-technology-may-adversely-alter-child-development

- "Play-Doh or iPads in Early Childhood?: Experts Say Both, But . . . "

  www.bamradionetwork.com/educators-channel/811-play-dough-or-ipads-in-early-childhood-experts-say-both-but

- "How Much Technology in the Classroom Is Too Much?"

  www.bamradionetwork.com/educators-channel/2239-how-much-technology-in-the-classroom-is-too-much

- "Is Technology Sapping Children's Creativity?"

  www.washingtonpost.com/blogs/answer-sheet/post/is-technology-sapping-childrens-creativity/2012/09/12/10c63c7e-fced-11e1-a31e-804fccb658f9_blog.html

- "A Silicon Valley School That Doesn't Compute"

  www.nytimes.com/2011/10/23/technology/at-waldorf-school-in-silicon-valley-technology-can-wait.html?_r=0

CHAPTER 24

The Homework Debate

Only recently has "schooling" come to be seen as the end-all-and-be-all for children and to be considered the most important part of their lives. The thing they require to become the individuals that adults want them to be (which is not necessarily the individuals the kids themselves want to be).

Our culture essentially holds kids hostage from early morning until late afternoon, to a great extent neglecting their need for true socialization, physical activity, play, quality time with parents, and for daydreaming and other creative pursuits. And these days, because academic achievement is held in such high esteem, our culture is intruding further and further onto the little time children once had for that "other stuff." Because, heaven forbid, children should have no time when they're not "learning," elementary school (and, in some cases, even preschool) students are being assigned more homework than ever—expected to continue their academic pursuits even after the school day has ended.

There's no lack of debate around the issue. Enter the word *homework* into the search box at BAM Radio Network, and you'll find no less than seven different segments on the subject. Etta Kralovec, author of *The End of Homework*, tells us that this particular debate has a long history, dating back to the 1920s and 1930s.

But one has to wonder why there's any debate at all, *when the research clearly shows no correlation between academic achievement and homework in elementary school.*

Perhaps worse, according to Sara Bennett, coauthor of *The Case Against Homework*, thanks in large part to this cultural habit, most kids over the age of eight aren't reading for pleasure any more, which is truly a sad state of affairs. Because they've been required to read and to do projects around their reading since prekindergarten, by the time they're in second grade there's no longer any joy for kids in the written word. That alone should be reason enough to put an end to the homework debate.

But, as they say on the infomercials: Wait, there's more! Homework has also been connected to loss of sleep, temper tantrums, and such physical manifestations as stomachaches and hair pulling.

How much healthier and happier kids would be if, as Sara suggested in a BAM Radio discussion, they could go home and do whatever they're interested in and then go back to school fresh the next day. But adults don't trust kids to know what's in their best interests. Nor do they place any value on downtime, especially these days, when being busy has become a badge of honor.

But let's think about downtime. When we allow a kid to just be, his creativity and imagination are sparked. A child with time to think—to ponder and reflect and simply let the mind go—will make up games, create dramas to act out, build a fort, or even dream up a way to contribute to the world. A child without such time develops only the ability to do what he's told, when he's told to do it. And that child isn't likely to become an adult with initiative.

Downtime also enables a child to find her strengths and weaknesses, her passions and talents. As she experiments with a variety of activities at her own pace and in her own way, she discovers her likes and dislikes. And when she has the opportunity to spend time on those activities she likes—to delve deeper into the possibilities—her interests and skills blossom.

Downtime allows children to spend time outdoors and to experience nature firsthand. Reports indicate that fewer than 10 percent of U.S. children currently learn about nature from being outside. Instead, one-third of them learn about it at school, and more than one-half of them learn about it via electronic devices such as computers and television! Richard Louv, author of *Last Child in the Woods*, who has coined the term "nature-deficit disorder," maintains that as children spend less and less of their lives in natural surroundings, "their senses narrow, physiologically and psychologically, and this reduces the richness of human experience." Indeed, to be human is to be part of nature. We evolved in the outdoors. And as much as we may have changed since our days as cave dwellers, our brains are still hard-wired for an existence in nature. We therefore have an innate link with it that when broken leaves a part of us bereft.

And then there's the value of relaxation, which is both a learned skill and a necessary one. Acquiring the ability to relax enables children to find a quiet place inside themselves that allows them to cope—to maintain control over their bodies and minds. The child who learns to relax will have the ability to manage stress and therefore lead a healthier—and more serene—life. But it will also ensure a more energetic life, as stress is most certainly an energy robber.

There's no debate over whether or not learning is important for kids. The thing is, they're learning all the time; it's just unfortunate that learning about such things as oneself, nature, and stress management are not considered as worthy today as are math equations and spelling words.

There are those who will say that doing homework teaches children such things as responsibility and delayed gratification. But the research in defense of these arguments is slim. To my way of thinking, kids get enough responsibility and delayed gratification during school hours. And even if the research were unequivocal, such traits could be attained in ways other than through homework—while the skills acquired from downtime are simply being lost.

Advocates for either side of the homework debate likely can find research in defense of their position. But there's no disputing the fact that once a person's childhood is gone, it's gone.

What's a Teacher to Do?

- To the extent possible, ensure that "learning" is done during the school day. Seven to nine hours of schooling is more than ample time for kids to be wrapped up in academics.

- Give homework assignments sufficient consideration prior to making them. Principal Brian Nichols stated in a BAM interview that homework is a "cultural habit" for teachers and parents. If that's your reason for assigning homework, it's not an adequate one. Brian suggested that you start with the question, "Why am I giving this assignment?" Is it going to be engaging? Does it enhance the learning that took place in the classroom, or is it simply busy work?

• Only assign homework that will take minimal time! Ignore such unfounded notions that you should assign ten minutes of homework per grade (e.g., ten minutes for first grade; twenty minutes for second grade; etc.). Sara Bennett points out that with distractions at home, ten minutes can easily turn into an hour. Josh Stumpenhorst, a teacher who believed in homework until he had kids of his own, further impugns the ten-minute rule, emphasizing that ten minutes for one child, who may learn at a slower pace or isn't capable of the same tasks, aren't equivalent to ten minutes for another child.

• If you're pressured by parents who believe that homework is essential to their child's success, take a page from Josh's book. He has an agreement with parents that during his time with their kids, he'll give them the most learning opportunities possible. He tells them, "When they are home with you, that is your time; do what you need to do as a family. I will respect your time and you will respect mine." He says that this arrangement has worked well, and he's had nothing but positive reactions to it.

• If you're pressured by administrators who believe homework is essential to academic achievement, point out that in Finland they assign very little homework (because they value the child's time out of school) and that country's test scores are exemplary. Brian Nichols also recommends that you talk with administrators about the work you're trying to do—the goals you're trying to accomplish—and how homework does or doesn't fit. This, he believes, will get you further than simply implementing a "no-homework" policy.

Where to Learn More

- "Homework? Really? That's So 1950s"

  www.bamradionetwork.com/educators-channel/971-home
  work-really-thats-so-1950s

- "How Much Homework Is Too Much?"

  www.bamradionetwork.com/educators-channel/115-how-
  much-homework-is-too-much

- "End Homework Now"

  www.ascd.org/publications/educational-leadership/apr01/
  vol58/num07/End-Homework-Now.aspx

- "Homework: An unnecessary evil? . . . Surprising findings
  from new research"

  www.washingtonpost.com/blogs/answer-sheet/wp/
  2012/11/26/homework-an-unnecessary-evil-surprising-
  findings-from-new-research/

- "Why Daydreaming is Critical to Effective Learning"

  http://blogs.kqed.org/mindshift/2014/10/why-daydreaming-
  is-critical-to-effective-learning/?utm_source=feedburner&
  utm_medium=feed&utm_campaign=Feed%3A+kqed%2
  FnHAK+%28MindShift%29

CHAPTER 25

In Defense of the Arts

A lot of what I read these days about education saddens me. But one of the saddest things I've come across lately was a piece in Valerie Strauss's column in the *Washington Post*. Its title was "Kindergarten show canceled so kids can keep studying to become 'college and career ready.' Really."

I'm certain she added that last word to the headline because such a thing is almost impossible to believe—almost. To anyone who's been paying attention to the current educational climate, this is stunning and sickening but not necessarily shocking.

Here's the letter, sent by the school's interim principal and four kindergarten teachers to parents upset by the cancellation:

> We hope this letter serves to help you better understand how the demands of the 21st century are changing schools, and, more specifically, to clarify misperceptions about the Kindergarten show. It is most important to keep in mind is [sic] that this issue is not unique to Elwood. Although the movement toward more rigorous learning standards has been in the national news for more than a decade, the changing face of education is beginning to feel unsettling for some people. What and how we teach is changing to meet the demands of a changing world.

The reason for eliminating the Kindergarten show is simple. We are responsible for preparing children for college and career with valuable lifelong skills and know that we can best do that by having them become strong readers, writers, coworkers and problem solvers. Please do not fault us for making professional decisions that we know will never be able to please everyone. But know that we are making these decisions with the interests of all children in mind.

It disturbs me every time I read it—for so many reasons. Among them is the clear implication that the arts are considered of so little significance as we prepare children to become "college and career ready" that even in *kindergarten* children are learning there are only certain skills worth having.

Let's look more closely at the letter, beginning with the statement that reading, writing, and the ability to work collaboratively and to solve problems are "valuable lifelong skills." I agree wholeheartedly. What frosts me is the idea that these skills are better gained by "academic" subjects and test-taking than through the arts.

What is the better way to ensure a love of the written and spoken word—being forced to read assigned stories, to memorize spelling words and definitions on which they'll be tested or bringing words to life through a play, or perhaps by writing poetry and songs?

What is the better way for children to prepare to become coworkers? Sitting at individual desks prepping for tests and then filling in bubbles? Or could it be by having them collaborate on a project that brings them joy and a sense of fulfillment?

The same can be said for learning to solve problems. I hardly think that being force-fed information that's later regurgitated on tests is the best way to acquire this skill. Instead, why not give students the opportunity to solve actual problems—such as those that might arise in the creation and production of a play?

How about the last sentence in that letter—about having the interests of *all* children in mind? Are they kidding? Are there not children with the potential and passion to go on to become brilliant chefs, landscape designers, master craftsmen, and architects or to become writers, painters, choreographers, composers, and actors? What will happen to their potential and passion when given no soil in which to grow? When the focus of their education has been "drill and kill?"

Is creativity (the ability to solve problems and to see beyond what already exists—and an essential element of the arts) not going to be required of our future scientists, entrepreneurs, doctors, inventors, and technologists? Is creativity not necessary in all aspects of life? How is it supposed to be fostered in students if all they've been taught is to follow directions—and that there is only one right answer to every question?

Further, how will today's students learn to look for and appreciate aesthetic beauty when it becomes clear to them *in their earliest years* that it's not valued? A life without beauty is nothing to aspire to.

Finally, there's the contention that the "demands of the 21st century" are responsible for this action. If ever there was a century demanding imagination and self-expression—both of which are nurtured by the arts—it's this one.

I honestly can't believe I have to argue these points; they seem like common sense. But, sadly, as I find myself saying on far too many occasions, common sense has gone the way of the dodo bird where education policy is concerned.

In an Edutopia piece, author Fran Smith writes,

> Years of research show that [arts education] is closely linked to almost everything that we as a nation say we want for our children and demand from our schools: academic achievement, social and emotional development, civic engagement, and equitable opportunity.

Yet again, policymakers are ignoring the research.

In a BAM Radio interview, Jennifer Stuart, a school art coordinator, asked "What do we value, and what kind of people do we want to have in the world?"

It's a great question—and one I think policymakers and education reformers ought to spend more than a little time pondering.

> ## What's a Teacher to Do?

- The simplest answer to the question asked in the heading is to incorporate art into your curriculum. You don't need to be artistic or consider yourself creative in order to do so. Children are naturally creative and will lead the way. You can also rely on the expertise of others in your community.

- Don't worry that including the arts may have a negative effect on test scores. Fran Smith's article quotes Tom Horne, Arizona's state superintendent of public instruction, who says, "If they're worried about test scores and want a way to get them higher, they need to give kids more arts, not less. There's lots of evidence that kids immersed in the arts do better on their academic tests" (if only every state had such a wise person in charge).

- Whenever possible, in as many content areas as possible, employ divergent problem solving so kids come to understand it's possible to have more than one "right" answer to a single question. For example, using manipulatives, how many ways can students demonstrate the number nine (possibilities include two groupings of five and four, two groupings of one and eight, and three groupings of three)? What are some alternative endings for a story just read? How many ways is it possible to demonstrate the effects of gravity?

- Allow students to do projects in ways that appeal to them. For instance, following a unit of study, let students choose how to demonstrate their understanding—whether it's by writing an essay, poem, or song; building, painting, or drawing something; or creating and performing a dance or a skit. Their excitement about these kinds of assignments will far surpass any you've seen about taking a test!

Where to Learn More

- "The Value of Arts in Education"
  www.bamradionetwork.com/educators-channel/448-the-value-of-arts-in-education
- "Why Arts Education Is Crucial, and Who's Doing It Best"
  www.edutopia.org/arts-music-curriculum-child-development
- "The Importance of Art in Child Development"
  www.pbs.org/parents/education/music-arts/the-importance-of-art-in-child-development/
- *Artful Teaching: Integrating the Arts for Understanding Across the Curriculum, K–8* by David M. Donahue and Jennifer Stuart

CHAPTER 26

No More "Good Job!"

When I taught a course called Movement Fundamentals as an adjunct at the University of New Hampshire, I invited children from a local child care center to come to the gym once a week to work with my physical education and early childhood majors. And once a week, at least a few dozen times, I'd hear the phrase "good job!" from my students, in response to something the children had done.

"Good job!" "Good job!" "Good job!" "Good job!"

Now, to those educators specifically taught to use praise and "positive reinforcement" to encourage kids—and to parents accustomed to saying "good job" for everything their children do, from eating their veggies to blowing their nose—it might have seemed that my university students were doing a *good job*. But I winced every time I heard it.

For one thing, as I explained to them, the expression isn't remotely informative; the children haven't a clue about what they've done that's "good." So how did that help them to improve?

Also, the phrase was often dishonest. The children didn't necessarily have to *do* a good job in order to be told they had. And you know what? The children knew it. Children can sense when adults aren't being honest, and the words become meaningless to them—so they tune them out. In a BAM Radio interview on the topic, the late Stanley Greenspan said, "If you drown a child in praise, nothing has meaning." He also said, "A parent who says 'Very good' or 'Terrific' every time a child burps is not providing genuine self-esteem."

Of course, my students weren't and aren't the only ones guilty of the tendency to overpraise and over-reward. I used to do it myself! Also, I hear and see it everywhere there's a mix of adults and children: in homes, on playgrounds, in classrooms, and even in the grocery store.

As I mentioned, preservice educators (particularly early childhood educators) are often instructed to use positive reinforcement with children. But Ellen Ava Sigler told me in a BAM interview that people tend to misunderstand what positive reinforcement is. She said, "They believe that positive reinforcement is sweets, treats, and empty praise, when positive reinforcement is positive attention. . . . [S]imply acknowledging a child's work or talking to a child about what they're doing *is* positive reinforcement."

With the so-called self-esteem movement of the last couple of decades, the confusion has only deepened. Somehow, adults have been led to believe that they must do everything they can to *give* children self-esteem.

While this belief—and the concept of verbally or physically rewarding children—may seem harmless, there are many problems with the idea of giving children self-esteem, not the least of which is that it isn't possible. You can foster it, but you can't offer it up like Thanksgiving turkey. Also, trying to bestow self-esteem through constant praise and rewards simply doesn't prepare children for the real world.

Sure, hearing "good job" the first few times—or receiving a sticker or a gold star—may make a child feel good. But the feeling is temporary. And *someone* is eventually going to critique or criticize her. Instead of a happy-face sticker or a pat on the back, a teacher or an employer is going to hand back a heavily red-penciled report and demand to know what she was thinking. Blue ribbons will not be awarded just because she walked through the classroom or office door. And no one is going to say "good job" unless she's actually done one. And even then she might not hear it. But the child who has come to expect extrinsic reward—who has become convinced that everything she does is worthy of praise or prizes—will be the adolescent or adult who can't handle life's realities.

Perhaps even worse, the self-esteem movement and its practices have resulted in what experts are saying is a link between instant gratification ("Thanks for coming; here's your blue ribbon.") and a lack of frustration tolerance in children. In Sharna Olfman's book *All Work and No Play: How Educational Reforms Are Harming*

Our Preschoolers, psychiatrist Marilyn Benoit notes that she's seeing a growing number of "explosive" children who are "unable to cope with the slightest of frustrations, and lash out aggressively. They are entitled, demanding, impatient, disrespectful of authority, often contemptuous of their peers, unempathetic, and easily wounded." And these are *preschoolers* she's describing.

But it also describes the teenage girl I witnessed, who clearly as a younger child had been made to believe she could do no wrong. Shocked, I watched as she threw a heavy, second-place trophy at the judge who'd presented it to her because, for her, first place was the only ranking that mattered. Being number two wasn't acceptable— but having a temper tantrum (at her age), and potentially injuring a judge, were.

This is not the kind of attitude we want populating the planet. So, yeah, I wince at the sound of "Good job!"

What's a Teacher to Do?

• First and foremost is the imperative to stop saying "good job" or, even worse, "good girl" or "good boy" (which implies the child is good because they are doing what we asked). Unfortunately, this is a harder habit to break than you'd imagine (believe me; I know), but awareness is the first step. If you're determined to stop saying it, you eventually will.

• I once heard a workshop leader say we have to stop "moralizing" by saying things such as "That was a good jump." Again, it doesn't tell the child anything. But if we describe the jump we witnessed as high, low, light, or heavy, we provide the child with helpful information.

• Similarly, say, "I notice" or "I see" instead of "I like." Name what the child *did*. For example, instead of "I like all the purple you used in that drawing" say, "I see you used a lot of purple in that drawing." If you accompany the statement with a facial expression and tone that convey pleasure, the child will feel rewarded but in a way that promotes intrinsic motivation.

- Avoid false praise at all costs. Not only do kids know it when they hear it; also, they know they're going to receive it regardless of what they do. For example, I once came upon an anecdote from a new teacher who used praise lavishly as a way to "win over the group." But when he later became frustrated because the class wasn't focusing, he chided them for not making enough effort. In response, one student said, "What's the point? You'll just tell us we did fine anyway." From the mouths of babes.

Where to Learn More

- "Rewards for Academic Performance: A Good Idea?" with Edward Deci

  www.bamradionetwork.com/educators-channel/465-rewards-for-academic-performancea-good-idea

- "Creating Praise Junkies: Are You Giving Children Too Much 'Positive' Reinforcement?"

  www.bamradionetwork.com/educators-channel/618-creating-praise-junkies-are-you-giving-children-too-much-positive-reinforcement

- "Developing Genuine Versus Phony Self-Esteem in Children" with Stanley Greenspan

  www.bamradionetwork.com/educators-channel/155-developing-genuine-versus-phony-self-esteem-in-children

- "Too Many Kids Quit Science Because They Don't Think They're Smart Enough"–an interview with Carol Dweck

  www.theatlantic.com/education/archive/2014/11/too-many-kids-quit-science-because-they-dont-think-theyre-smart/382165/

- "Five Reasons to Stop Saying 'Good Job!'" by Alfie Kohn

  www.alfiekohn.org/article/five-reasons-stop-saying-good-job/

CHAPTER 27

Bribes and Threats Work, But . . .

Some time ago, I was doing movement activities with a group of five-year-olds. I wanted them to stand straight and tall but, following the philosophy of movement education, I didn't want to simply *tell* them to stand straight and tall. Instead, I asked them to imagine their bodies were like tree trunks reaching from the ground to the sky—and that their feet were like the trunk's roots, securing them to the ground and keeping them steady.

Suddenly, one little girl angrily announced, "I'm not in the Army!"

Whoa. I was stunned. Where had that come from? And what was I supposed to say or do in response?

Remembering my early childhood studies, I turned to another child who was standing precisely as I'd envisioned. "That's exactly right!" I exclaimed. "You're standing so nice and straight and tall!" And when I looked back at my little dissenter, she too was now standing straight and tall because she too wanted to be rewarded with praise.

Blatant manipulation? Absolutely. Still, I never thought of it that way until I heard Alfie Kohn give a speech based on his book *Punished by Rewards*, at a conference. He passionately explained that rewards and punishment are actually mirror images of each other, both used for the purpose of getting kids to do what we want.

I remember debating with myself during the two-hour drive home. Was there something different that I should have done with my little "soldier"? Was it absolutely necessary that she stand straight and tall? In the end, there was one conclusion I couldn't avoid: I had rewarded one child with praise in order to control another.

Many years later, Edward Deci told me in a BAM Radio interview that "praise is all too often used by people as a way to control kids." Of course, by that time I was solidly on his—and Alfie's—side, having read *Punished by Rewards* and a great deal of research demonstrating that neither "bribes" nor threats are effective in the long-term for either behavior management or building character and fostering intrinsic motivation.

In fact, there's *so much* research determining the ineffectiveness—the *detriment*—of using rewards and punishment that it's hard to imagine why any teacher or parent would continue to employ them or why any preservice program would continue to recommend their use. But they do.

Not long ago, in fact, in an online forum, a teacher asked, "Is it okay to bribe your students?" I was fascinated and dismayed by the responses. While an overwhelming number of teachers objected to the word "bribe" (insisting that "reward" was a more appropriate term), they did indeed think this was a great practice because it helps "prepare kids for the real world."

Just as the little soldier's comment had stopped me in my tracks so, too, did that one. Apparently the belief is that rewarding kids is no different from adults receiving bonuses for a job well done in the "real world." The contention disturbed me, so I gathered together some experts for another BAM Radio interview and posed the following question: Is "rewarding" kids similar to adults receiving bonuses for a job well done? What was Dan Pink's response? "I think it is similar, and I think it's similarly ineffective."

Dan, the author of *Drive: The Surprising Truth about What Motivates Us*, calls these kinds of things "if/then rewards": if you do this, then you get that. He explained that 50 years of social science tell us they *are* effective as performance boosters *but only* for simple tasks "with very short time horizons." He added,

the same body of research tells us they are far, far, far less effective for work that requires judgment, discernment, creativity, conceptual thinking, and for work that has a longtime horizon.

There's nothing inherently evil about if/then rewards; it's just that if we really want our kids to be creative, conceptual thinkers— have longtime horizons and not be . . . just mice chasing after the next bit of cheese, then we have to abandon our heavy, heavy, heavy reliance on if/then rewards in all circumstances.

Dan maintained that the evidence is "overwhelming" that these practices do not work and in some cases even have "collateral consequences that ought to terrify us."

When I asked the remaining panelists why the research is being ignored, they—teachers all—agreed that it comes down to compliance or the quick fix. And they admitted that achieving compliance is easier than getting engagement—the latter of which is what keeps kids motivated.

Teacher Josh Stumpenhorst asked, "Are you trying to create compliant students or engaged learners?"

Early childhood educator Deborah Stewart wrote in an e-mail sent to me following the interview, "just know that the best way to get children to listen, care, and respect each other and you is to capture their attention and get them engaged. A compliant child may make your job seem easier, but an engaged child will make your job rewarding."

Amen.

Instant gratification, "easy," and "it's always been done this way" aren't good enough reasons to keep bribing or punishing kids if we're truly concerned about their future and the kind of human beings we're helping to mold.

What's a Teacher to Do?

• Deb Stewart recommends that we condition ourselves to refrain from starting any sentence with the words "If you . . . " when we want students to get things done.

• Josh Stumpenhorst suggests giving students tasks and assignments that are worthwhile to do, as this is what motivates them (listen to the interview to hear what he says about Innovation Days and Passion Projects).

• Don't make rewards such as stickers, stars, and pizza parties part of your classroom culture. Instead, make *choice*, which is a necessary ingredient in fostering intrinsic motivation, something the kids can come to expect. For example, if you want the students to do an art project, allow them a choice of materials. If you're assigning a writing project, give them a choice of topics.

• Like choice, *enjoyment* contributes to intrinsic motivation. If you want the children to move desks and chairs, play a fun piece of music and challenge them to finish before the song ends. The task then becomes associated with fun. If you join in, the sense of togetherness adds to the experience.

• If you do praise children, do it sparingly (children can become praise addicts), and always be sure the praise is both honest (not used to control but to congratulate) and deserved. For example, when a student has responded in a kind and generous way to another student in need: "You did a wonderful job of making [Lee] feel better."

Where to Learn More

• "Classroom Management: Yes, Bribes and Threats Work But . . ."

www.bamradionetwork.com/educators-channel/1066-classroom-management-yes-bribes-and-threats-work-but

• "Punished by Rewards? A Conversation with Alfie Kohn"

www.ascd.org/publications/educational-leadership/sept95/vol53/num01/Punished-by-Rewards%C2%A2-A-Conversation-with-Alfie-Kohn.aspx

CHAPTER 28

Time to Give Time-Out a Time-Out

Once upon a time—whether it was in the home or in the classroom, with a hand, paddle, or ruler—spanking was the norm. It was simply how children were disciplined. Then the experts determined that there are a lot of valid reasons *not* to spank. Eventually, time-out was created as an alternative. It has since become the most popular form of discipline among parents and early childhood educators. Even teachers at higher grade levels, although they probably don't use the expression "time-out," employ this discipline when they remove a student to the back of the classroom or to a chair in the hall.

But is time-out a good solution?

I used to think so. If ignoring misbehavior didn't work and the child's actions were potentially harmful to herself or others, I'd remove the misbehaving child to the sidelines. But because I thought the one-minute-per-age rule was arbitrary and ridiculous, and I wanted the child to take some responsibility, I'd always say, "Let me know when you're ready to rejoin us." I thought that was brilliant—until one day a boy walked to the sidelines, said "I'm ready," and walked right back to the group. So much for that policy.

The conventional thinking—and it surely was mine—is that time-outs are harmless enough, certainly as compared with spanking or whacking with a ruler, and they give the child an opportunity to think about what he's done to deserve separation. But, more often than not, the child isn't thinking about what he's done; he's either having a pity party or forming a deep resentment. More often than not, power struggles are the result of time-outs—especially considering how overused they tend to be.

More important, according to Dr. Peter Haiman, a guest on BAM Radio and a child therapist who's conducted an extensive review of child-rearing research, time-outs damage trust, which he says "is probably one of the most important things for learning."

Of course, if one is thinking of discipline in terms of punishment, then time-outs fit the bill. But discipline shouldn't be about punishment; it should be about children learning to make better choices. And that's not likely to happen when a kid is continually being stressed.

Dr. Haiman contended that separation is the worst thing that can happen when a child misbehaves—in fact, that's when the child most needs to be close. And Daniel Siegel and Tina Payne, authors of *No-Drama Discipline*, agree. They've written that children have "a profound need for connection . . . particularly in times of distress." They state,

> Even when presented in a patient and loving manner, time-outs teach [children] that when they make a mistake, or when they are having a hard time, they will be forced to be by themselves—a lesson that is often experienced, particularly by young children, as rejection. It communicates to kids, "I'm only interested in being with you and being there for you when you've got it all together."

Brain imaging, they say, shows that experiences of emotional pain—such as feelings of rejection—look very much like those of physical pain in terms of brain activity. Such experiences, when repeated often enough, can actually change the brain's physical structure.

Even if time-out is not used as punishment but, rather, for the purpose of helping the child calm down, it can still generate a negative effect due to the isolation and to the fact that time-outs usually involve sitting still—which does *not* come naturally to children. While many parents and educators believe this is an opportunity to teach a child with a lot of physical energy self-control, the more likely outcome is frustration, fidgeting, and additional stress. A child with a lot of physical energy typically needs to expend energy in order to calm herself. Moreover, self-control can't be imposed; it has to be attained, and that won't be possible if resentment, lack of trust, and misery are present.

I've come to accept that as a blanket strategy, time-outs are overused, misused, developmentally inappropriate, and harmful. Just like spanking had its day so, too, has time-out. It's time we gave this practice a permanent time-out.

What's a Teacher to Do?

• There's no doubt that children will sometimes need a break. We all do. In a Responsive Classroom (see information cited below), the children are prepared beforehand for such breaks. They know that the break is not punitive; rather, its purpose is to restore focus and control. Implementing a similar policy at the beginning of the school year can help reframe the idea of time-out for your students.

• Don't refer to these breaks as time-out, which has come to be associated in children's minds with punishment. Even "positive time-out" won't do the trick. Instead, you can call it "Take a Break," as they do in Responsive Classrooms. Or you might ask the students to come up with a creative title for them.

• Daniel Siegel and Tina Payne recommend taking a "time-in," during which you sit with the child and talk.

• Allow children to take their own breaks, as needed.

• If you're going to suggest that a child take a break, it's going to be most beneficial *before* any misbehavior—when you can sense the child is about to lose control.

• Don't introduce a timer into the process; it only invites power struggles.

- Allow children to find their own ways of calming themselves. Jody Johnston Pawel, in the aforementioned BAM interview, suggested that they might need to do something verbal to calm down. They might need to do something expressive, such as artwork. They may have to do something physical, such as squeezing a ball or even running around on the playground. Some children may even need to be near you in order to calm themselves.

Where to Learn More

- "Time to Give Time-Out a Time-Out"

  www.bamradionetwork.com/educators-channel/666-time-to-give-time-out-a-time-out

- "Replacing Time-Out: Part One—Using Guidance to Build an Encouraging Classroom"

  www.naeyc.org/files/tyc/file/Gartrell%2001.pdf

- "What Is Responsive Classroom Time-Out?"

  www.responsiveclassroom.org/article/positive-time-out

CHAPTER 29

"You're Outta Here!"

If time-out leads to feelings of isolation and unworthiness (and it does), imagine how it feels to a child to be thrown out of school—often for reasons he or she can't even fathom.

Attorney John Whitehead wrote the following in a piece for the *Huffington Post*:

> What we are witnessing, thanks in large part to zero tolerance policies that were intended to make schools safer by discouraging the use of actual drugs and weapons by students, is the inhumane treatment of young people and the criminalization of childish behavior.

Certainly these examples, cited previously in this book, qualify as "childish behavior":

- a seven-year-old biting his strawberry Pop-Tart into the shape of a gun;
- two 6-year-old boys playing cops and robbers during recess and using their fingers to make imaginary guns;
- a six-year-old making a gun gesture with his finger, pointing at a classmate, and saying "pow"; and
- a five-year-old girl telling another girl she was going to shoot her with her pink Hello Kitty toy gun that discharges bubbles.

Attorney Whitehead cites others in his article, including

- a nine-year-old with a LEGO person holding a 2-inch toy gun (in honor of his father, a retired police officer);
- an eight-year-old wearing a hat to school decorated with an American flag and tiny plastic Army figures carrying miniature guns (in honor of American troops);
- a seven-year-old bringing a NERF gun to school;
- a 12-year-old doodling on her desk with an erasable marker; and
- an eighth grader wearing rosary beads to school (in memory of her grandmother).

Childish, right? That is to say, this is the kind of behavior that children, given their age and experience, can be expected to exhibit. I mean, who among us hasn't played cops and robbers? Pointed toy, handcrafted, or imaginary guns at childhood friends and watched as they pretended to be shot, falling to the ground in dramatic fashion? Who among us as a child hasn't wanted to hold tight to a treasured item or succumbed to the desire to doodle? These actions weren't deemed "criminal" then; nor should they be now.

How shocked and horrified would we have been if we were hauled into the principal's office, interrogated by a group of grownups looming over us, and then thrown out of school and isolated from our friends? Perhaps even dragged off in handcuffs? I can't imagine the terror I would have felt as a child in such a situation. But those were exactly the consequences meted out for the "infractions" listed above.

Such stories should incite the ire of everyone who reads them. So should the fact that the rate of expulsions in state-funded *preschools* has been found to be more than three times higher than the national expulsion rate for students in kindergarten through Grade 12.

Now, I'm not going to pretend that I think all preschoolers are angels; I once taught a group of four-year-olds whose antics stopped me from working directly with kids for *three years*. But I have to wonder how there could be such large numbers of little children who have done something so wicked that they're tossed out of school.

And to what end? As Dr. Walter Gilliam told me in a BAM Radio interview,

> The children who tend to benefit the most from a high-quality early education program are the children who are in greatest

need of it. And if there's ever a child who's in good need of a school readiness experience it's a child who has behavior problems in a classroom.

Consider, too, that not only do the punishments not fit the crimes, they also can't be considered logical consequences. As Laura Bornfreund points out in another *Huffington Post* article, unless the "discipline focuses on teaching children how to act appropriately, they won't learn anything from it." And isn't learning how to behave—to be ready for school and society—the whole point behind early education?

Zero tolerance policies and school expulsions, especially in the early years, are two practices that *really* make me wonder if administrators and policymakers understand—or even like—children. Zero tolerance policies and discipline that only intimidates, terrorizes, and teaches children that they are unworthy to remain among their peers, simply have no place in education.

What's a Teacher to Do?

• Insist that you and your colleagues be offered training in the management of challenging classroom behaviors. This is the type of training most often requested by teachers—and most likely to be lacking.

• Get to know each child in your classroom, and make an effort to connect with the children's families. Dr. Gilliam told me he's never seen a child expelled from a preschool classroom where the teacher and the parent had a good relationship. He said,

> If the teachers know the parent, know the family's story, know the child's story, they seem to be so much more able to connect with the family, to be more tolerant of the child's behaviors, and much more likely to work with the child over time.

• If your school has a zero tolerance policy, lobby against it—with administrators, school board members, and parents.

• Think in terms of logical consequences. In other words, the punishment must fit the crime. Laura Bornfreund used the example of 2 six-year-old boys suspended for getting into a food fight in the cafeteria. Rather than suspension, which is more likely to cause confusion and/or defiance, Laura submitted that being required to clean the tables in the cafeteria would have been more instructive.

• If you're in an early childhood classroom with access to mental health consultants, make use of this service. Preschool teachers with such access reported far fewer incidences of students acting out.

• Be cognizant of your own levels of stress and burnout. Dr. Gilliam reported that teachers who screened positive for depression expelled students at twice the rate of those who did not screen positive—and that job stress was an even better predictor "above and beyond depression."

Where to Learn More

• "Why Are Preschool Expulsions Rising?"

www.bamradionetwork.com/naeyc-radio/201-why-are-preschool-expulsions-rising-rapidly

• "Why Suspension Makes No Sense in the Early Grades"

www.huffingtonpost.com/laura-bornfreund/why-suspension-makes-no-s_b_1369554.html

• "Zero Tolerance Schools Discipline Without Wiggle Room"

www.huffingtonpost.com/john-w-whitehead/zero-tolerance-policies-schools_b_819594.html

• "Schools Must Abandon Zero-Tolerance Discipline"

www.edweek.org/ew/articles/2014/07/24/37mediratta.h33.html

• *Implementing Policies to Reduce the Likelihood of Preschool Expulsion*

http://medicine.yale.edu/childstudy/zigler/350_34772_eKExpulsionBrief2.pdf